ide

gay life

www.thegoodwebguide.co.uk

dedication

For Jo

thegoodwebguide

gay life

Jonathan Carr

The Good Web Guide Limited • London

First Published in Great Britain in 2001 by The Good Web Guide Limited

Broadwall House, 21 Broadwall, London, SE1 9PL

www.thegoodwebguide.co.uk

Email:feedback@thegoodwebguide.co.uk

Original series concept by Steve Bailey.

10 9 8 7 6 5 4 3 2 1

A catalogue record for this book is available from the British Library.

ISBN 1-903282-13-6

The publishers and author have done their best to ensure the accuracy and currency of all information in this volume, however they can accept no responsibility for any loss or inconvenience sustained by any reader as a result of its information or advice.

Project Editor Michelle Clare

Design by Myriad Creative Ltd

Printed in Italy at LEGO S.p.A.

contents

the good web guides

The World Wide Web is a vast resource, with millions of sites on every conceivable subject, where cyber-communities have grown, and people have formed relationships, and even married on the net.

However, busy people want to use the internet for quick access to information, rather than spending hours on end surfing; it can be a quick and useful resource if you are looking for specific information.

The Good Web Guides have been published with this in mind, and to give you a head start in your search, our researchers have come up with a collection of reviews of the best sites around.

Our recommendation is impartial ; reviews are focused on the website and what it sets out to do, rather than an endorsement of a company, or their product. A small but beautiful site run by a one-man band may be rated higher than an ambitious but flawed site run by a mighty organisation.

Relevance to the UK-based visitor is also given a high premium: tantalising as it is to read about purchases you can make in California, because of delivery charges, import duties and controls it may not be as useful as a local site.

Our reviewers considered a number of questions when reviewing the sites, such as: How quickly do the sites and individual pages download? Can you move around the site easily and get back to where you started, and do the links work? Is the information up to date and accurate? And is the site pleasing to the eye and easy to read? More importantly, we also asked whether the site has something distinctive to offer. On the basis of the answers to these questions, sites are given ratings out of five. As we aim only to include sites that we feel are of serious interest, there are very few low-rated sites.

Remember: the collection of reviews you see here is just a snapshot of the sites at a particular time. The process of choosing and writing about sites is rather like painting the Forth Bridge: as each section appears complete, new sites are launched and others are modified.

As this is the first edition of the Good Web Guide, all our sites have been reviewed by the author and research team, but we'd like to know what you think. Contact us via the website or email feedback@thegoodwebguide.co.uk. You are welcome to recommend sites, quibble about the ratings, point out changes and inaccuracies or suggest new features to assess.

You can find us at www.thegoodwebguide.co.uk

introduction

People used to have to go out to experience the pleasures and pains of the gay scene; now they can get it all in the comfort of their own home. It may be that you want more pleasure, or that you want to escape some pain, or that you are simply looking for something else. That 'something else' is often on the internet, and revealing it to you is what this book is all about. Many bars and clubs are better in their on-line form than in reality – where they are full of unappealing men, filthy toilets and drag acts performing the same routines they were doing in 1979. Nor can you ever check your bank balance, play blackjack, order CDs, download Napster's music or do a Sainsbury's shop from your local gay club. No dear, not even from DTPM. From within your gay internet experience, you can, and you don't have to squabble over mini cab fares afterwards either.

This book reviews the gay on-line world: the chat rooms where you can find men to have sex with, bitch with, humiliate or just simply disconnect; the online stores which sell the goods to which gay men have traditionally aspired, like poppers and Viagra; the bar and club sites, the porn and sex sites, the personal web cam sites, the health sites, and just about everything else. The plan is not just to tell you what is out there, but also how it works, what you can expect, and whether anyone behind it is committed to quality, to turning you on, to showing you something you hadn't seen before, or even just to acknowledging you as a fledgling homo-surfer who has hit the gay bar ceiling and wants something new. So, what is this world like?

As far as health goes, the wealth of information on-line now is overwhelming, and its presentation is often excellent. Features like Aidsmap.com's The Wheel, which assists HIV positive individuals in planning when and how to take their pills, epitomise the Internet's provision of services and concepts that you simply can't find anywhere else. If you can get what you want from a television or a newspaper, or even from a doctor, then it's hard to see the point of the Net; but of course you often can't get what you want from your doctor – how would he know about the latest research into African prostitutes with AIDS? – with the Internet, you can find out.

Celebrity pages are often hugely entertaining. With a spend of hundreds of thousands of dollars, sites by Warner Bros on behalf of Madonna, for example, are often clever, revealing and well-designed. The Internet is where some celebrities feel they can address the world without having their thoughts interpreted by the media. Shopping is in many ways a far superior experience online, and the personal sites fan out into a tour of sexuality that you can begin whenever you wish; one which you can explore, interact with and laugh at, all at your own pace. There isn't anything else in life, I don't think, that quite so effectively serves the anonymous, voyeuristic, reptilian part of the human brain. And you need to take care of all the bits of your brain, don't you?

My most enjoyable experiences in the gay on-line world came from the chat rooms, where you can organise a sex party in ten minutes - sometimes, even, a good one. In these rooms a brutal (but sensible) picking up system is in force. Because they do not have to deal with you personally, some users choose to fire their unwanted negativity at you: just remember to defrag your hard drive afterwards and you'll be fine. If you do decide to meet someone in the flesh common sense always applies. A quick phone call before you give out your address should speak volumes about what's likely to happen.

The chat rooms and the sex are what the Internet is about for a lot of people, but there is nothing cheap and easy about Internet sex. The holy grail of the gay.com room is the man who is good-looking, sexy, nearby, prepared to travel and who, when he arrives, looks exactly like his horny pic. He rarely exists, but if you do happen to be him you will have a lot of fun here. Prepare to have windows shut in your face constantly if you are someone else. Gay.com is really the ultimate in sloth, and therefore it is what gay men have been after for years. Cigarettes helped me to get my sloth up to full power. You'll probably need something!

For many gay men the sex chat room will be where they start and stop thinking of the Net as 'gay'. The argument about what makes something 'gay' is something best left to New Labour, and so I have mainly chosen sites which chimed with my heart, gut or cock. A lot of people in businesses all over the world have put a lot of effort into making the Internet fun, cool and interesting and, though they have failed, their attempt is well worth seeing. Images, art, design and writing capabilities that soar above the standards of television and newspapers are now commonplace, and they are yours virtually free.

Whatever can be said for and against the Internet, the function it has for gay men is very simple. Here, in a homophobic nation lacking any likeable gay role models, and with a gay scene whose energy is locked, who wouldn't appreciate an alternative? It may be solitary, it may be a time sink, and it may drive you mad most of the time, but it is a change. It is another pathway to changing how you feel, for a short time. So, open the book, take a holiday from reality, plug yourself in and have a look around toy world. If you like it, plunge right in! Get a webcam. Get a faster PC. Get a bodi-tek machine so you can work out while you surf. Get it on! The gay scene will still be there when you want to show it a good time. And - this is my appeal to the world following my Internet investigation – if you don't have an eight inch cock, please, please, don't tell people that you do. Because that, my friend, is what is holding your computer future back. Enjoy!

Jonathan Carr, February 2001

internet tips

your kit

Always buy the best computer equipment you can afford. It goes without saying that you should get a screen guard (and ground it to eliminate static), position the screen at eye level (stack it on old phone books if you have to, just don't look down at it!), and have the keyboard low enough so your elbows are at a right-angle as you type and click. Put your feet on the floor and take 10 minutes break for every hour of computing. If you want to perfect your computing or office environment you can do more. An air ioniser and a couple of spider plants will deal with the static negative ions and ozone that computer and printing equipment can produce, and something as simple as keeping the desk completely clear tends to be relaxing and enables you to surf more effectively.

your connection

Current Internet sites often use Shockwave Flash and are designed to run on Pentium III computers with a 56k v.90 standard modem. You should get a connection from your ISP of 36,000 to 46,000 bps, and that's as fast as a 56k modem gets. Checkout deals like BT Together and Home Highway, and deals on second lines because there are many options. NTL offer a new package to get you online, which is very competitive, and other companies like Telco and Cable and Wireless have their own services. You should not be paying more than 1p a minute now for daytime surfing with anyone.

If you are with BT, use Surftime. If you use the off-peak version, which is £5.99 per month, connect during the day with a company such as LineOne, which has a 1p per minute dial up and no ISP service charge. Then put your LineOne internet connection number in Family and Friends to save 10% off your 1p per minute call each time you go on-line. In the evenings and weekends, connect with Surftime.

Of course, Surftime is the BT deal, but you still need an account with an ISP. Undoubtedly the BT Surftime offer of £5.99 per month for evenings and weekends and £19.99 for 24 hour unlimited access is the best deal (at the time of going to press). To set up your account you will need to obtain a Surftime number from BT, which you can get by quoting your customer reference number and phone number on the www.bt.com site. You then give this number to one of the participating ISPs and they will open an account for you. You download the software and connect with the new access number given you by the ISP. If your telephone number is ex-directory you must enter 1470 and a comma before the dial up number in order to make Surftime work. It is useful to know details like this in advance because if Surftime doesn't work, you will have to call technical support. They will charge you up to £1 a minute for the privilege, so it pays to figure out your question clearly before you call. Once the service is running you don't need to call the premium number again: just email your question to customer services and they are obliged to respond. Not every ISP is participating in Surftime. For example, ISPs which are already free of charge, like LineOne, do not seem to qualify. Therefore, you may need a new ISP. Choose one of the providers which does not make an additional service charge on top of the Surf time fee. The best at the moment is Freeserve, which even gives you a rebate of £1 per month, bringing the off-peak Surftime fee down to £4.99. Most of the others make additional charges which make a mockery of the Surftime price-saving invitation. The worst offender I found for this was PlusNet, which shrewdly charges £5.99 a month for its service. This figure, identical to the Surftime fee, seduces you, into thinking that you are paying once when in fact you are paying twice. Using a company like Freeserve the only charge you will see for your off-peak Internet use is the Surftime fee on your phone bill. Remember, when you set up Surftime there's no need to get rid of your old connection. For example, you could connect with LineOne in the day at 1p a minute and Surftime with Freeserve during evenings and weekends, and get the best of both worlds. The only downside here is that you will perform a search for new mail using Outlook Express using one connection or the other, and you may not be able to get the messages from LineOne when you're connected with Freeserve. Still, you can get them next time you go on with LineOne.

your privacy

Before you start delving into the Net you would be wise to ensure that your computer is properly secure and that your privacy is protected. One tip for privacy is to wipe your user details in Internet Options. Many Internet users have entered their full address and telephone numbers during registration, and these details are then visible to anyone who clicks on your email properties when they have received something from you. Wipe your details to preserve your online anonymity. Some people worry about fraud online but the basic legal fact is that if someone nicks your credit card details and uses your card fraudulently, it's no different from their taking your actual card and using it in a shop. If you are a victim of fraud it is most unlikely that you will be in any way liable for money spent without your consent, and apart from the standard legal reasons why this is the case, nobody wants to see Internet commerce collapse, so consumers are virtually guaranteed protection. On the other hand, NEVER use another person's card to make purchases online, even if they have given you permission.

software

A great site for new patches, upgrades and free software is www.updates.com which will automatically scan your computer to see what is out of date and then allow you to download upgrades and fixes from all kinds of different companies. If you are losing your connection while online or if you have had a virus on your system, you should be able to sort these things out with updates. New software is coming out all the time, which you can download from many sites. Additionally, you will probably need to download Shockwave Flash, RealPlayer, Realdownload and a Zip package in order to take full advantage of what's on-line. If a site is using these programs it will typically link you to another site where you can download the software. Virus software, unlike these other programs, is not free and it is essential since some viruses are capable of wiping your hard drive and they cannot be seen until it is too late. Of the many on-line options some of the most useful are online backup programs, which are usually free, the free online email programs like hotmail, which can be accessed from any PC. Among the most useless are links which offer to 'speed up' or 'optimise' your Internet connection. These don't work, and things won't go any faster.

payment

If you want to be paid for the time you spend online you could try www.alladvantage.com. You will have to put up with a one-inch high advertising bar on your screen, in return for which you will be paid a small sum of money related to how much time you spend surfing.

getting organised

The 'My Favourites' section of Internet Explorer is there to help you organise the chaos of the web. As you accumulate more sites you enjoy visiting it's worth spending an hour filing your sites in your own folders like Food, Money, Shopping and Travel, rather than having a long list of sites which fills the favourites page. Surfing should be as pleasant as possible and there are few things more annoying than trying to remember a page you went to once which you now can't find!

cookies

If you are online frequently your computer will become increasingly full of 'temporary internet files' like cookies and all sort of stored elements from the pages you have visited. There is no harm at all in any of these things although you can refuse cookies if you like. The point of a cookie is to identify you to a site when you go online and they are the reason Amazon.co.uk, for example, always know it's you when you arrive at the page. These temporary internet files do take up hundreds of megabites of memory, however, and it makes sense to wipe them once in a while. This process should be in addition to ordinary maintenance like scandisk, defragmenting the hard drive and emptying the recycle bin.

just in case...

And finally, in the event of a thunderstorm, disconnect from the Net and switch off your computer - lightning strikes can upset the delicate circuitry of your modem, and your computer company will not replace it for you free of charge in the event of this kind of damage. There's another contract you haven't read . . .

acknowledgements

I would like to acknowledge Elaine Collins, and everyone at the
Good Web Guide who worked on this book.

user key

£   subscription required

R   registration required

🔒   secure online ordering

UK   country of origin

lifestyle

What is a gay lifestyle? When all is said and done, it probably isn't that much different from any other lifestyle, except it doesn't usually involve marriage or children and often involves a greater degree of emphasis on sex. But we're already making sweeping generalisations. Beyond the sexualised world of the gay scene, which finds its counterpart online, gay men do the same kinds of jobs, live in the same kinds of houses and moan about the same things as everyone else. In this section we focus on the online 'gay scene', a world of chat rooms, porn sites, picture galleries, escort agencies, postcard and video vendors, and personals sites. But there is also a world of professional associations, clubs and sports organisations, online soap operas, fascinating legal sites and the like. We'll begin with the most familiar service from the modern internet: the sex chat rooms!

gay

overall rating: ★★★★★	
classification: lifestyle	
updated: continuous	
navigation: ★★★★★	
content: ★★★★	
readability: ★★★★★	
speed: ★★★★★	
US R	

www.gay.com
Gay.com

If you venture online you will have found chat rooms, and those at Gay.com are the best. But there is a lot more to Gay.com than just chat rooms; it is, after all, one of the biggest gay lifestyle sites online. First up are the day's features, which could be about anything and are usually well-written pieces of journalism: interviews, articles, competitions, TV guides – the lot. Then there's the Gay.com Headline News, which brings you gay goings-on from around the world, whether it's a bomb blowing up a gay bar in Cape Town, a gay police officer winning an employment tribunal in Holland, or the House of Lords getting very hot and bothered about the thought of having sex with a 16-year-old boy. Then you've got your Resources, which amount to people offering you inaudible long-distance phone calls at 0.0001 cents an hour to distant gay cities (like Brighton). And if that isn't enough, there are the spin-off Gay.com sites in France and the UK, since Gay.com is a US site, and Gay Shopping, via which you can book seats on American Airlines flights, or buy a book at Barnes and Noble online.

It's all too much! So you need the Site Map, which shows you where to find Food and Wine, HIV life, the relationships channel and the money section. Gay.com is like a huge magazine, the kind that you'd need a car to bring home. Which is fine, because you're already at home.

SPECIAL FEATURES

Catch of the Week A sexy male and a sexy female presented for your drooling delectation. The person is usually gorgeous, intelligent, talented and young, and thousands of miles away in Washington State.

People Explore this section to find the message boards, which reek alternately of sex and loneliness (the same thing, possibly), to learn about the chat service before you dive in, or to join a community. There are plenty to choose from, including communities devoted to coming out, leather, transgender, women and youth.

Shop Witness vendors lining up for your pink coppers. They've seen you coming, they know who you are, Amazon have sold them your credit card details, the name of your cat and your star sign – and they are ready to pounce. There are links to Banana Republic, Beauty Jungle, Gap, Saturn (cars), and American Airlines. Buy a video or go to the pharmacy.

My Gay.com This is where you tinker with your account, tell them where to forward your emails, spray paint your homepages and work on your profile. Would you pick yourself up? Here's where you find out.

HIV Life This section should grab your attention because, instead of pumping out information about HIV and AIDS (not a bad thing in itself), it gives personal stories from people who are coming at HIV from different angles. Some are men, some are women, some were diagnosed in the early 1980s and some have just found out, some are on meds and some are not. These stories are often courageous and moving, and they make a change from AIDS information sites (see Health).

Arts and Entertainment Everything you need to know about film festivals, US TV shows and books. Gay.com has partnered with the New York Times to bring you book reviews of some of the current bestsellers online. Profiles of stars abound, with Sandra Bernhard, Lynda Carter and Joe Jackson being among those having their say.

Chat For a brilliant internet sex chat experience, this is the authentic version. Advertising is hardly noticeable while you are online, and instead you see a screen full of chat rooms and your private boxes. It's really seductive. Choose from a list including UK and Ireland. Within that category are rooms for every part of the country, and other specialist rooms. There are five main rooms for London, then London Central, East, North and so on, but the specialist rooms attract men from all over the country. People are whomever you want them to be – as long as they don't actually come over, that is! Bold users write Gay.com intros and put their photographs online, so that you can click on them and see what you're in for, usually by examining a single image at facelink.com. Visit www.facelink.com to set up your own image in minutes. More timid participants reveal only their name, location and stats, and you must then talk them into trading pics. The experience of trading pics, which is like waiting for your credit card to be authorised, can bring up a raft of weird new emotions. As your unconscious fights with the brutality of the scenario, your conscious mind will try like hell not to take it personally when you are declined! Then it's time to decide: will you 'accom' or 'travel', do you have 'chems' or 'poppers', Viagra or spliff, or are you (oh my god) a timewaster? On Gay.com you can even set up your own page, filled with pictures, information, your horoscope and your take on life, though why people insist that they are 'masculine and funny' is beyond me. The terrible thing about the Gay.com chat room is that it does bring out the worst in people (not that Trade is much different, come to think of it). Once the impatience sets in, it's all downhill. As you click the meaningless, picture-less names in the middle of the night, you will soon find (though it might take you a while to admit it to yourself) that anyone who doesn't have an eight-inch cock and an online picture of his perfect body, and who can't rush over right now, armed with cocaine, becomes a total bore. And yet, when was the last time anyone with a great body and an eight-inch cock was willing to rush over to your house at three o'clock in the morning with cocaine? See? Thinking with your cock doesn't work. Have fun, see you there.

Bigger than The Bible and a lot more fun. You'll never leave. You are now an internet hermit.

overall rating: ★ ★ ★ ★ ★
classification: finance
updated: daily
navigation: ★ ★ ★ ★ ★
content: ★ ★ ★ ★ ★
readability: ★ ★ ★ ★
speed: ★ ★ ★ ★
UK

www.massow.co.uk
Ivan Massow's Money Company

You may have followed the Mr Massow story as he has progressed through his various incarnations of good looking gay person, on to very busy financial gay person, on to millionaire gay person and now, New Labour gay person. The entrance to this site is presumably meant to raise a smile. It shows an office whose doors are fronted by a red carpet, and asks you to click here for an exciting entry to the inside of the palace. Otherwise you can click on the dingy side gate 'for a very unexciting HTML experience'. OK. Well, you need shockwave flash,that's what he means. Then, wait while Ivan unlocks the office. It does take an age to open, but when it does, it's quite spectacular – a blond wood floor with a fur-coated Sony electric dog on it, a ferociously expensive red desk on which a computer sits, real traffic noise, a bouncy rock toon, and images of the employees. Nice sofa, Ivan. Click around the room on the various things to get more information. For example, if you click on the documents on the desk you are shown the Massow customer form, an amazing piece of detective work which you should fill out on your company's time. It may come as a surprise to you that 19% of Massow's clients earn £18,500 a year or less, so you may be able to take full advantage of financial services even if you didn't think you had enough money coming in. Read the terms of business and then have a click around.

SPECIAL FEATURES

History This room contains all the press on Massow, and a database of press articles about money. You can search for what you want (enter a search word like cash or ISP), read it there or have it emailed to you.

Finance News Click on the newspaper and you see a list of articles, such as: 'Endowments, are they all they're slagged off to be?' , 'Tax returns are worth returning.' and 'What is the Pink pound?' The advice is clear, well-written and thought provoking though it could do with a bit of editing. Massow, who has written these pieces, comes across as a highly intelligent man who appears to occasionally become self-conscious about the seriousness of what he's doing, at which point the articles veer away from clear advice into his own personal take. I can't say whether this will make his business more appealing to you (a personal touch?) or more irritating, since he is, after all, a businessman dealing in financial services. Nevertheless, I don't quibble with free financial advice, however it is presented.

Playroom Kill Mr Pinstripe. What does that mean? Well, load up your birthday cake and find out.

People These excellent self-written profiles are a chance for the employees (shown as cardboard cut-outs around a boardroom table, again on that blond wood floor) to tell you something about their qualifications, experiences and lives.

Services Scrawled on a whiteboard, these; no doubt an attempt to make them seem less intimidating, though even Ivan is unable to make the idea of choosing a pension glitter with a high level of fun and excitement. Once again, the advice is so clear, detailed and fresh that even Gordon Brown would learn something if he read it. There is advice here on investments, life assurance, mortgages, pensions, corporate benefits, health insurance, general finance and critical illness. Books on the floor guide those with questions about HIV. This section is very rich and definitely repays study if you are HIV and should be read even if you are considering a test – something that I have never heard THT, Lighthouse, GMFA or the testing counsellors ever mention. Print it out. Presumably customers are left to their own devices to figure out the financial advantages of signing up to the www.stanleyacropolis.com casino and cutting out the new McDonald's vouchers for 99p Quarter Pounders.

A fascinating, beautifully designed site, with interlocking parts and fun things to do, as well as the serious matter of how to manage your money and protect your future. Makes you want to read The Economist.

www.gay365.com
Gay 365

Gay365 is a mauve lifestyle page which you will either fall in love with or despise. Light, fluffy, strangely heartening and featuring both its own soap opera – of which you can become a part – and membership options, it is Daniel Pashley's latest venture into the gay internet. Your browser won't fill up with images of naked men here, which makes the site refreshing and, sadly, almost unique! The design is sensible and fun, and the site's membership grows by the day. Readers are encouraged to send in their views and comment on whatever Gay365 is interested in this week – like who are Britain's sexiest footballers – but you can write to them to express yourself about anything you like.

SPECIAL FEATURES

Latest A kind of news service, though you won't catch them telling you that the Northern Ireland peace process has broken down or that Concorde has got some new pink tyres. You're more likely to learn which Big Brother contestant has signed a deal with L'Oreal or what's up in Doll Babylon (see below). Tips on marketing yourself, online etiquette and deciding what you want are good. The political reports from Oliver Branch, MP, are truly excellent, and surprising, and in spite of painstaking research I still don't know whether this is a real person or a character. Madonna's baby made the news, there's a Big Brother quiz, and the archive is crammed with the best recent articles.

overall rating:
★ ★ ★ ★

classification:
lifestyle

updated:
daily

navigation:
★ ★ ★ ★ ★

content:
★ ★ ★ ★ ★

readability:
★ ★ ★ ★

speed:
★ ★ ★ ★

UK   R

Doll Babylon Doll Babylon is a still-picture soap opera with dolls in place of actors. All the back episodes are online but, like a real soap, you can join the story at any point. It's like Photo-Love, except with a real plot and some very funny lines. New episodes appear every Monday. The gist of it is that evil landlady Morag plots endlessly against her tenants, while Switch lunches with the Duchess in the Rainbow Lounge and recovers from her alien abduction. Aspen seeks help locating his missing penis but winds up making a date with his doctor. Meanwhile, Poppy and Julian are set to be a doll boy band and Biff gets a blow job in the bushes from a married man. You're hooked already, aren't you?

Culture/Scene This covers just about everything! When we visited the site, they'd done a tasty review of DNA magazine and an interview with its editor. Next up was a dissection of kids' TV shows, including the finest of all, Rainbow, and an analysis of the camp, classic kids' shows Mr Benn, Perils of Penelope Pitstop and He-Man. A surprising interview with Peter Tatchell followed this, followed by a detailed review of The Witches of Eastwick (stage version) and a report of a 48-hour club rave in Ibiza which left you wondering why you're not there the whole time instead of in Blighty. Excellent stuff, with plenty to read that's well-written, fun and not too serious.

Humour How gay are you? Take the Gay365 online quiz and find out. Beneath the tongue-in-cheek exterior, there's a more interesting undercurrent of melancholy and despair here – many a true word spoken in jest, eh boys? Elsewhere, the page's agony aunt, Shirley, straightens out readers on issues such as the secrets of a long-lasting relationship.

The Wire The Wire is Gay365's meeting place, and it's free to use. You can become a member in seconds and a photo of a current member appears on the left each time the main page loads or refreshes. My god, you could be famous, darling!! The Wire is wonderful, as long as you don't mind the fact that you leave footprints everywhere as you use it. If you look at someone's page, they know. If someone looks at your page, you know. If a third party looks at your page, they can see who has been looking at you as well. Interesting, eh? It's all very incestuous and clever. Profiling is intelligent, since you must choose between options, but it gets irritating after a while. As usual, images help enormously – really, why would you send messages to men whose appearance you don't know? Perhaps people are afraid of being seen in the strange, new online world. The search tool is great: it tells you where the person is and whether he has a picture online. I searched for 'sex', 'arse' and 'cock' initially, to see where that got me. Of course, if you search for 'sex' you get people from Essex. Oh dear.

The Gay 365 Team Daniel Pashley explains that the site aims to be the most entertaining online space for gay men in the UK, and he pledges to never forget that you have a brain as well as, presumably, a cock.

A fun, imaginative site that deserves to succeed.

gay

overall rating: ★ ★ ★ ★	
classification: sex and lifestyle	
updated: continuous	
navigation: ★ ★ ★ ★ ★	
content: ★ ★ ★ ★ ★	
readability: ★ ★	
speed: ★ ★ ★ ★ ★	

UK R

www.gaydar.co.uk
Gaydar

If Gay.com is the current chat room standard on which most others are based, Gaydar is probably the site which does the best job of interactive personals. There's a news service powered by rainbownetwork.com but organised slightly differently, and a secure shopping server with a small selection of goods. Nevertheless, there is no disguising the fact that the true purpose of the site is to deepen your contractual relationship with the Devil and get you having sex.

SPECIAL FEATURES

Design your own page Once you have carefully read yet another sheet of terms and conditions (yeah, right), you may graduate to Gaydar Slut in moments. Tell them where you are (Gaydar operates in The Netherlands and South Africa, among other foreign-type places) and fill out the huge form. This page of information is not necessarily what you want broadcast to the world, and you don't have to fill it all out. Just project yourself however you want. Some of the guys who have filled out profiles on Gaydar do not seem to regard it as a self-selling exercise, but what else could make any sense as an approach? In a world of entirely interchangeable sex partners, what have you got that makes you worth selecting? Do remember, though, that a lying tongue is one of the seven abominations before the Lord (Proverbs 6:6-19). One suspects that this extends to the keyboard.

Gaydar allows you to upload five photographs, which can feature nudity, erections or whatever you like. A further set of private photos can be uploaded to your private area and sent out rapidly while you're online. When you are online you get a list of everyone who's there, and everyone has an address for instant mail and a line explaining what they are looking for. Mostly, people say they are 'browsing' but then few things are called what they really are these days! It's the same as how arrogance is now known as 'self-esteem'. Once you're online you can search the user database, store messages, identify friends and cupids, and see who else is online. The Gaydar assistant lets you know what's going on. Typically, on a weekday night in London, about 200 to 250 guys are on this site, looking for sex. The real question is whether Gaydar is exciting, fun, rewarding or full of hot guys. In a word, no – but I'm sure you'll find out for yourself.

Upgrade Upgrade to Gaydar Gold or Platinum for a range of additional services. Platinum membership is £60 for a year. The extras are listed on the screen.

The interactive men's messaging service.

overall rating: ★★★★	
classification: lifestyle	
updated: continuously	
navigation: ★★★★	
content: ★★★★★	
readability: ★★★★	
speed: ★★★	
UK	

www.rainbownetwork.com
Rainbow Network

From the adverts in QX, which showed two silver-painted women surfing, we assumed that Rainbow Network was one for the ladies. Almost all printed material which announces itself as 'gay' is about the needs, desires and thoughts of gay men (this web guide being no different), and this bias exists on the web. However, Rainbow Network seems to be even-handed about meeting the needs of gay men and lesbians. The main page opens with news and navigation boxes to The Arts, Predictions, Music, Travel, News and Scene. Beneath these you can select Chat rooms, Personals, Classifieds and Forums. It's a very extensive site with minimal advertising, well-presented news items and polls, plus the editor's views about gay life at the moment. As with all of these sex/lifestyle sites, you can become a member, log into the page and thereby personalise the way the page functions somewhat. The only problem I noticed with Rainbow Network is that each and every page is crowded with items to load, making it a comparatively slow-loading site. Still, the popularity of a page like this rests on the quality of the writing more than anything, and I thought it was excellent. Journalism that is worth reading is not something you find frequently on the web, but this page worked.

SPECIAL FEATURES

Dyke's Digest Mercedes, the Women's Editor, tells you what's going on in the UK lesbian world. This section presents the site's current articles and introduces you to the high standard of writing on Rainbow Network, not forgetting its sense of humour.

News At the time of review, there were ceaseless Madonna stories, news on homophobia cases, a landmark asylum case, and the somewhat embarrassing conviction of a former Stagecoach executive for soliciting a male prostitute in Texas.

Arts, Predictions, Music News Here's where you'll find full-length reviews of the latest books and music, along with competitions and your horoscope. The page headlines something (like Armistead Maupin's latest book) and then takes you into a pretty overwhelming selection of additional subsections. For example, sub zones in 'the Arts' include books and poetry, previews, profiles, gossips, interviews and the diary of a kept boy.

Travel Guides At the time of review, Montreal's lesbian life was the focus of the travel guide, and the one-page article presented was excellent – concise, interesting and, most importantly, enough to make you want to visit the city.

A strong site with a lesbian focus, presenting news, financial information, health advice and chat.

overall rating: ★ ★ ★
classification: lifestyle
updated: every weekday
navigation: ★ ★ ★ ★ ★
content: ★ ★ ★ ★ ★
readability: ★ ★ ★ ★ ★
speed: ★ ★ ★ ★ ★
UK

www.spiceupyourlife.org.uk
Spice Up Your Life

If you can bear the occasional lapses into bitchiness, this site will give you heaps of information about gay everything: gay shopping, press, hotels, support groups, personals, holidays and an Amazon book search on the entry page. It's not very exciting visually but the site excels in its aim to give you information.

SPECIAL FEATURES

Gay Resources The resources index is particularly good, with details of Gay switchboards, gay social groups, UK lesbian and gay organisations, HIV and AIDS organisations, student groups, solicitors, coming out groups, national gay groups and even organisations who do gay and lesbian weddings. There are also guides to UK Pride and gay events, online shopping, Wimbledon tennis, email and chat abbreviations and London's internet cafés.

Gay Press A short guide to everything that is available along the lines of gay press and publications, including QX, Boyz and Attitude. A link takes you to a page where you can order a subscription online.

Gay Radio Details of current gay and lesbian radio shows.

Personals A large selection of free personal ads to browse, or you can add your own. Requires membership. There is also a

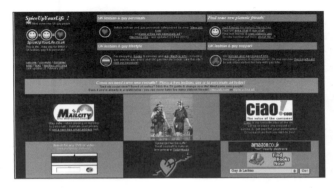

chat service featuring dyke chat, gay chat and, for platonic friendships, Just Friends.

Books A large selection of gay goods, guides, postcards, lesbian fiction, biographies, Time Out Guides and a special section devoted to Patricia Cornwell. Also, erotica and film books.

Gay Hotels A guide to gay hotels nationwide and a link to the London Holiday Accommodation Bureau.

A neatly presented site which gives you loads of information.

OTHER SITES OF INTEREST

Lesbian and Gay Police Association
www.lagpa.org.uk
Formed in 1990, the Lesbian and Gay Police Association was set up after a group of Police staff in the Metropolitan Police, London, realised the need for some kind of network amongst gay or lesbian officers. Since the initial social event, it has grown to include members in nearly every UK Police Service. They offer advice and support, and work towards equal opportunities for lesbian and gay police service employees, and better relations between the police and the gay community.

Bar Lesbian and Gay Group
http://meltingpot.fortunecity.com/kings/245/
BLAGG was set up by four Bar School students in 1994, and has since gone from strength to strength, now boasting over 400 members. BLAGG tries to offer friendship, advice, support, accommodation for those students outside London intending to dine at the Inns, a social network, and a voice at Bar Council meetings and Government department level. The group is open to lesbian and gay barristers, pupil barristers, student barristers, law students, barrister's clerks and others connected with law. If you want more law associations, a full list is to be found at www.infolaw.co.uk/ifl/assoc.htm

London Lesbian and Gay Switchboard
www.llgs.org.uk
Calm words 24 hours a day about love, life, safer sex and practically everything else. The London Lesbian and Gay

Switchboard can also give you phone numbers of regional switchboards in England, Scotland and Ireland.

The Site
www.thesite.org

The Site is designed to connect young people, principally in the UK. It gives the best information, help and advice available and hosts a comprehensive list of gay, lesbian and bisexual websites and organisations.

Gay Business Association
http://www.gba.org.uk

The GBA was established in 1984 by a group of business men and women who saw the need for a professional organisation which could improve standards, share information and experiences and promote gay business generally. As part of the gay community, they have grown in stature and confidence in recent years. Similar organisations representing gay business were well established in the United States. Now associations of gay businesses are taking root in the rest of Europe. By coming together in this way, and building a network of business contacts both here and abroad, gay men and women are able to give practical expression to the idea of the pink economy.

Gay Airline and Travel Club
http://members.tripod.com/~gatc/

The Gay Airline and Travel Club is for gay men who are interested in travelling, meeting guys, seeking travel companions, collecting airline memorabilia or working in the airline or travel industries. It has some lovely pictures of planes and a quarterly newsletter with free personals, all the issues of which appear online. This site, run by a US airline worker, usually offers fantastic deals on air travel – but bear in mind that it's a US site. You'll have to get there first.

Viajar Travel

http://www.viajartravel.com

This site claims to be 'the web's ultimate guide to gay and lesbian travel adventures', and it includes travelogues about Lima, Peru, Gay Puerto Vallarta, Hiking the Inca Trail and Cuzco, Peru. So forget about Mykonos and read this lot! Viajar readers send in accounts of their travel experiences, which vary from the horrifying to the magical, and you can read them online. The site is well designed and packed with photos, advice and news.

Bearhug

http://www.bearhug.het

This is Bearhug's intro: 'a social group for gay men whose primary interest is Bears. No, not the furry, cute type you see in the zoo, but the hairy homosexual kind – anyone who is a Bear or a Bear admirer is welcome to join the club. We are based in London and currently have 425 members, mainly from around London...' You can join up, enter the Bear Ring for more sites, get details of upcoming events and buy merchandise. There's also an ad for The Bear Handbook, again available from Amazon. Check the gallery to see images of the recent parties.

Rank Outsiders

http://www.rank-outsiders.org.uk

Rank Outsiders is a support group for gay, lesbian and bisexual armed forces personnel, both past and present. Sponsored by Direct Connection, it provides professional and dedicated support to serving and former personnel, along with specialist advice for those dismissed or discharged on account of their sexuality and for those seeking re-enlistment to one of the three services. It also provides a social network. You can make a donation, look at the gallery, and read the sorry tale of the Ministry of Defence, the European Court of Human Rights and the personnel who never stopped fighting for their recently recognised rights.

Gay Bikers Motorcycle Club
http://www.gaybikers.demon.co.uk
I love this simply for the initial icon of a motorcycle being ridden to (what I imagine is) a naughty destination. Although they are slightly dangerous, motorcycles symbolise modern freedom much better than a Nissan Micra and prove Aldous Huxley's point that 'speed is the only modern pleasure'. Think about it. The GBMC was formed in 1977 and now has nearly 500 members, men and women in the UK and abroad. Order the magazine, get a provisional licence and a 50cc bike, sign up, or sweat over the pictures. Lovely.

Gay Classic Car Group
http://www.battenburgcake.com/gccg
Okay, so you can't quite bring yourself to take a motorcycle helmet into a gay bar and you want a proper stereo in your vehicle. Try the Gay Classic Car Group, then. The site's a bit boring to look at, but it is fun. There's a quarterly newsletter, Big End, and the Group has a number of Regional Reps throughout the UK to assist with local events and host local meetings. Once again, a Nissan Micra is not a classic car, even if it is 10 years old,

and the aim of the site is to fill you with enthusiasm for E-type Jags and the like. Membership figures are up to about 320 and growing, and the classic cars come to Pride to be shown. How awful it is to have one's gay stereotypes disrupted in this way!

Lesbian and Gay Employment Rights Page
http://www.lager.dircon.co.uk

The Lesbian and Gay Employment Rights page (LAGER) is a guide to employment issues. General advice is offered along with a review of the law, links, and online newsletters. If you have trouble at work there is a section to offer you advice. This is a useful site for anyone with work problems that are due to sexuality.

Military Resource UK
www.military-uk.net

You can find news on the UK's MOD lifting its gay ban, along with housing advice, information on all the forces, employment advice, veterans and stacks of other things you won't necessarily expect here. This site has links to all the official British Military sites, including the Marines, TAs, Royal Marines Reserve and Royal Air Force Auxiliary, as well as the main three. There are also maps of the former Yugoslavia and the Balkans region, and MOD links on the Kosovo crisis. A brilliant resource for anyone involved with the forces, or who wishes they were.

British Fire Service
http://www.fire.org.uk/others.htm

This site offers massive links to everything to do with fire and the fire service. There's even a link to a company that supplies breathing apparatus, should you fancy a weird night in. To read minutes from meetings, see a gallery of photos or join up, follow the link to http://website.lineone.net/%7Eflag.ship/ for the Fire Brigades Union Gay and Lesbian Support group.

Mondo
http://www.cplus.fr/html/courts/cveg-us/html/pride/euroccid.html
The original version of this site is in Français, but you can read it in an English version here. It tells you when all the Pride events in Western Europe are taking place, and it also carries political news from all our Euro partners.

AOL
http://www.aol.co.uk/webcentres/lifestyle/gay/
This is the massive AOL resource for gay men and lesbians. It has its own list of 'top five' sites and it offers gay and lesbian resources for all. News, a chat service and many cool links make this another great place to get a feel for the possibilities of the web. The 'How Do I?' section is particularly good, since it takes you directly to the answers you need.

Eurogay
http://eurogay.co.uk
Fabulous photo galleries aren't the half of it on this site, which also offers news, entertainments, reviews of over 850 gay movies, a search for Eurogay homepages and an editorial, which at the time of reviewing discussed cyber relationships and how old hat they are now. Eurogay also offers talk & date, a net search and images from Pride and Mardi Gras.

Queer Resources Directory
http://www.qrd.org/www/world/legal.html
This excellent site covers the legal issues that face gay men and lesbians. It offers the text of partnership laws in Denmark, Norway and Sweden, along with Australia's domestic relations bill. It also features information on the WHO's Global Programme on AIDS, immigration issues, non-discrimination and a list of ages of consent that are currently in force in the EU. Read the list of countries that criminalise homosexual sex before you book that flight to Cyprus.

University of Chicago Library
http://www.lib.uchicago.edu/~llou/sexlaw.html
This site features articles on Sexuality, Gender and the Law, outlining what the international laws are. It's a massive and well-organised site, offering many surprises to the UK citizen.

Age of Consent
http://www.ageofconsent.com
The name says it all. A site explaining the development of the age of consent worldwide.

The Knitting Circle – Law
http://www.sbu.ac.uk/~stafflag/law.html
This site, dubbed The Knitting Circle by its creators at the South Bank University, is a Law Centre with many links to sites and articles dealing with legal issues that affect gay men and lesbians. It's hugely interesting and thorough, and covers the various laws passed and repealed since the Buggery Act of 1533, which describes the '...detestable and abominable Vice of

Buggery ...', and goes on to define it as a felony punishable by hanging until dead. The statute was re-enacted in 1536, 1539, and 1541 under Henry VIII. It was repealed in the first Parliament of Edward VI, along with all the new felonies established by Henry, re-enacted in 1548, and repealed in 1553 with Mary's succession. It was again re-enacted by Queen Elizabeth I in 1563, and subsequently became the charter for all criminalisation in the English-speaking world. In England, only a few executions are known during the two centuries that follow. However, a series of polemical pamphlets, such as John Dunton's The He-Strumpets (1707) and the anonymous Satan's Harvest Home (1749), began to stir up public opinion against the homosexual subculture that flourished in large towns. So it didn't all start with the Stonewall riots, you see.

Sports

The Knitting Circle – Sports
http://www.sbu.ac.uk/~stafflag/sportsclubs.html
Lists sports clubs and organisations that are of interest to gay men and lesbians.

London Health
http://www.londonhealth.co.uk/sportsleisureclubs.asp
The London Health site allows you to search your postal area for private and local authority facilities, including pools, gyms, playing fields, tennis courts, women only centres, adventure playgrounds, and pitch and putt courses. It also lists London sports clubs and has a further section specifically for lesbians and gay men.

UK Gay Sports Festival
http://www.gaygames.org/TeamUK/uk2000_2.htm
Everything you need to know about the UK Gay Sports Festival
2000.

Gay Outdoor Group
http://bi.org/~goc/
Homepage of the gay outdoor group. This nationwide group
organises walking and specialist activities.

Goslings Sports Club
http://www.bigfoot.com/~goslings_cycling
Gay and lesbian sports body which offers badminton, swimming
and cycling.

Long Yang Club
http://www.longyangclub.org/london/badminton.html
A badminton club for Asian players and their friends.

Team Scotland Badminton Club
http://www.teamscotland-bc.co.uk
Homepage of the Team Scotland Badminton club.

Stonewall FC
http://www.stonewallfc.org
The Stonewall footie club, with over 100 members and, would
you believe it, talent!

Frontrunners
http://www.frontrunners.org
Global gay and lesbian runners' organisation with a large
membership.

Eurogames
http://eurogames.ch
This is the official site for the organisers of the second biggest
gay sports festival, which is being held this year in Zurich.

Gaysport.org
http://www.gaysport.org
Site in English and Dutch which brings together gay and lesbian
European sports lovers. Listings of tournaments and clubs.

Gay Games
http://www.sydney2002.org.au/index.html
Site for the next Gay Games.

British Gay and Lesbian Sports Federation
http://www.laga.org.uk/sports_fest/bglsf_&_team_uk.htm
BGLSF, the British Gay and Lesbian Sports Federation, seeks to
raise the profile and promote the interests of gay and lesbian
sports people in the UK, promoting participation in sport and
active recreation in order to enable them to fulfil their potential
as participants, coaches and officials.

Fired Up For Snow
http://www.firedupforsnow.com
A lovely new website dedicated to gay people into outdoor
sports, especially winter sports.

Religious groups

Integrity
http://integrityUK.org
Goes like this: 'The group and its activities were developed in

response to the particular issues raised for lesbians, gay men or bisexuals who are or have been evangelical. We strive to provide a place where people with this shared history can feel relaxed and at home. We will not impose evangelical theology or views of sexuality. Integrity is open to anyone who feels that they will benefit from its ethos.'

Alliance of Christian Churches
http://accnet.org

The Alliance of Christian Churches is a fellowship of churches ministering God's unconditional Grace both in the gay and lesbian community and the body of Christ at large. The website is for all who understand that the Gospel of Jesus Christ is for everyone.

Bridges
http://www.bridges-across.org

Bridges across the divide provides models and resources for building respectful relationships among those who disagree about moral issues surrounding homosexuality, bisexuality and gender variance.

Evangelicals Concerned Western Region
http://www.ecwr.org

The Evangelicals Concerned Western Region is a nationwide ministry of Christ-centred, Bible-believing, evangelical gay, lesbian, bisexual and transgendered Christians. ECWR is not a church, but a network for groups of friends whose primary purpose is to provide reconciliation, integration and opportunities for Christian growth among Christian GLBT peoples.

Gay Christians
http://www.gaychristians.org
Gay Christians is a network of friends around the world. The position they take is that there is no sin in homosexuality. The membership draws support from a great variety of faith traditions, and its strength from the richness of that very diversity.

Queer Christians
http://www.geocities.com/WestHollywood/Heights/4577/
Queer Christians is a group for people, especially younger people, who have some interest in church and church-related activities, and feel that they don't fit the usual sexual stereotypes.

Quest
http://www.users.dircon.co.uk/~quest/
Quest is an organisation for lesbian and gay Catholics in the UK. It exists to help reconcile faith and sexuality, offering social events, support and information.

Reconciling Ministries Network
http://www.rcp.org
The Reconciling Ministries Network (RMN) is a growing movement of United Methodist individuals, congregations, campus ministries, and other groups which publicly welcome all persons, regardless of sexual orientation.

The Safety Net
http://www.geocities.com/WestHollywood/9381/
The Safety Net is a group of lesbian, gay, bisexual and

heterosexual Christians who run the Safe Space every year at the Greenbelt Arts Festival, UK.

The Shepherd Initiative
http://www.shepherdinitiative.org/

This is how they put it on their opening page: 'The Shepherd Initiative is a diverse coalition of Christians affirming the dignity and integrity of all people by virtue of their divine creation; regardless of gender, race, religion, age or sexual orientation. We seek to begin to inform the public discourse on homosexuality from a Christ-centred perspective.'

Gay search pages
http://www.gaytoz.com

The UK's largest search engine for gay stuff. Enter a key word and off you go!

sex

When you think of the internet, I bet that you never think about trying to use it for sex. Oh no. You want books, darling, from that Amazon place you saw on the telly. You want to do that Tesco shopping thing you got a leaflet on the other day. You want to send flowers via those nice Interflora people in Barclay Square. You'd never dream of just typing S-E-X in your browser (it's a search string, darling, not a G-string) to see what happens, with your husband's, son's or boss's credit card quivering in your sweaty mitts, scratching your head and wondering just why sex is the most frequently typed search string on the net. Who are these people? Aren't they interested in NASA?

Well, this isn't real sex; that's the tedious, thumping and time-consuming thing you can't be bothered to do any more. This is the easier, safer and less laborious pretend sex, and it involves sex pics, sex films, sexy jpegs, expensive Manchecks that never seem to take you anywhere and steamy monitors that flicker with invitation. It's sex chat, sex fantasy, and sex lying-through-your-goddamn-teeth. Sex online. And it's fun, so wipe down your keyboard, let's go.

overall rating: ★★★★★	
classification: sex	
updated: weekly	
navigation: ★★★★★	
content: ★★★★★	
readability: ★★★★	
speed: ★★★★★	
US	

www.barebackjack.com
Bareback Jack's Page

Spooky music introduces you to this site, which is devoted to the fashionable but dangerous practice of bareback gay sex. It's a pay site, but one year's full membership is a piddling $4.95 – and the site is funny, sexy, interesting and realistic. It takes about a minute to sign up, and you can then take full advantage of the site's stories, pictures, message boards and 8-inch plus club. Mr Bareback Jack is based in Arizona, but that doesn't stop him from having sex with everyone all over the world and making a website to tell you all about it. If you want to know more about barebacking, this is the best website to click onto. It is incredibly rude and frank, and well designed.

Of course, the whole site is dedicated to barebacking, and barebacking can lead to infection with HIV. Nevertheless, people are free to do what they like, and here's where that and a whole lot more besides gets said. There's an FAQ section, an opportunity to send in your picture to Hot Desert Nights so that it can be considered for their next porn flick, scenes from the videos that won the bareback awards last year, and a rant against the homophobic Dr Laura.

SPECIAL FEATURES

Bareback Contacts Choose from bottom, top and versatile men all over the world, who you can then email with your stats and pictures. Also, there is a list of hot homepages of guys all over the world.

Real Men Galleries Investigate Jack's Polaroid gallery for pictures of guys at it, along with links to their homepages and email addresses set against the kind of stimulating backdrop you won't find in the John Lewis wallpaper department. Send in your own pictures for inclusion in the Gallery. Galleries include the Latin Love Lounge, World's Biggest Cocks, 8-inch plus club, Foreskin Gallery and Felching Gallery.

Information Jack discusses the risks of bareback sex and why men might choose to do it, retails expensive bareback videos (watch a preview in Media Player), and tells you about himself, his sexual practices and his page. He says: 'don't think that because I currently live in Phoenix I'd be so cruel as to recommend the place.' You can also find links to the bars he likes, his dungeon party pics, and information on his views, plus a hysterical section on accurate penis measuring that comes complete with a How To picture guide. Remember guys, only measure the actual usable penis and don't include the two inches of airspace in front of it! Also, there are notes on those who have mistakenly measured the unusable area of their cock.

Hot Stuff Funky shrine by Jack to JP Pitoc, a gorgeous film star who Jack has named the sexiest man alive. Do take a look (but don't rent Trick, Pitoc's godawful movie), and then submit dirty stories, follow the bareback discussion, send a postcard or learn about AIDS vaccine trials. The links are good.

Probably the least dishonest and funniest internet site about barebacking.

overall rating: ★ ★ ★ ★ ★	
classification: sex/lifestyle	
updated: daily	
navigation: ★ ★ ★ ★ ★	
content: ★ ★ ★ ★ ★	
readability: ★ ★ ★ ★ ★	
speed: ★ ★ ★ ★ ★	
FR	

www.projetx.com
Projet X

No, it's not a typo, it's Projet X. French for Project, comprend? This page, written in three languages, is a guide to the leather scene across Europe. And by Europe, they don't just mean Britain, The Netherlands and Germany; they mean all of it, all the way to Finland, Iceland and Prague. Better than the average guide, this site gives you a good idea of what to expect from these places (it seems that the writers have actually been there) and events they're likely to have on in the future.

SPECIAL FEATURES

Editorial There wasn't anything as strange for me, when I came out, as backroom bars, saunas, sex clubs and cruising areas. I couldn't make head nor tail of it. The people who write the editorial here can't either, and they have the courage to say so: 'Why is it that at any fuck bar there are twice as many people in the backroom than in the bar? Is it easier because that way you can hide from the scrutiny of others and yourself?' Very perceptive. In the multi-layered addiction that is gay sex (unless you are very unusual and fell in love as soon as you came out), there are many quiet mysteries to unfold. The editorial is good, and makes this page worth a trip.

Fixtures In the event that Europe is a playground to you, and you can take the Eurostar or a flight whenever you fancy it, this page is a must. All the clubs in Berlin, Paris, Amsterdam and so on are listed, and you can find out what is happening in them on each night. Places such as Hamburg, Eindhoven, Prague, Frankfurt, Milan and Rotterdam all have their own fuck bars where you can go for sex. Addresses are given.

Links A good links page, with private sites and links to photography and video sites of various quality.

A first-class guide to European fornication.

overall rating:
★ ★ ★ ★
classification:
sex/lifestyle
updated:
daily
navigation:
★ ★ ★ ★ ★
content:
★ ★ ★ ★ ★
readability:
★ ★ ★
speed:
★ ★ ★ ★ ★
UK

www.all-man.com
All Man

This useful site has a gay guide to 23 countries which covers clubs, bars, hotels, accounting services, escort agencies, tattoo artists, music, piercing, mini cabs, vehicle sales and everything else. You can get your horoscope, investigate the free galleries, send a postcard or shop. The online dating service is a message service, and although the low number of entries suggests it might be new, it does cover the whole world.

SPECIAL FEATURES

Galleries An excellent free gallery with some really hot guys. There are plenty of categories to choose from, including hunks, Latinos and bears. Images are fast-loading jpegs which you could use to sell yourself online – be prepared to have your legs broken, though, when your eager date turns up and learns the truth!

Postcards Send an online postcard to Tony Blair. Choose from Gay, Great Painters of the World, Male Celebrities, the Natural World and the Past.

Shopping This section, created in conjunction with Clone Zone, sells everything you could need to be completely gay, including special offers on aromas and lube, videos and DVDs, CDs, hard core magazines, clothes and swimwear, and toys and books. SSL shopping cart service is available and delivery charges are low.

A well-developed and sexy site with full news, shopping and gay guide services.

overall rating:
★ ★ ★ ★
classification:
fun/sex
updated:
daily
navigation:
★ ★ ★ ★ ★
content:
★ ★ ★ ★ ★
readability:
★ ★ ★
speed:
★ ★ ★ ★ ★
US

http://www.celebpecs.com
Celebrity Pecs

With more than one million hits in a short space of time, Celebrity Pecs have obviously hit a niche in the market. You have always been able to get their images on news servers like alt.celebrities, but those links often take you to paying porn pages and are a waste of time. Presumably noticing this, Celebpecs have gathered everything together for free. Most of the male stars you can think of are here, along with a few from US TV who you probably won't know. The page divides into galleries. Some stars, such as Mark Wahlberg, have dozens of pictures posted up in standard thumbnail and large formats; others have just a few. The page designers know there are loads of images of these guys on the internet, so there are always at least a few you won't have seen before.

The page opens with a banner of thumbnails of the major players in the perfect pectoral game. As with most things, it often happens that the famous don't possess the most perfect bodies (and who knows how many retouching operations these images have been through?). And yet there is always something compelling about them, be it the curve of a smile, the positioning of a nipple or the crunch of a bicep.

SPECIAL FEATURES

Celebpecs Update Here's where you'll find the new kids on the block, like Dylan McDermott from The Practice, Taye Diggs,

Ginuwine, Sisqo and Usher. Then there are the old men. Tom Cruise has just been added, along with Oz tennis star Pat Rafter and Mario Lopez from Pacific Blue. Each time you choose a name you are taken to the person's Fact File, where all kinds of tittle tattle can be gleaned, none of it sensational. You can click to Amazon to buy their movies, CDs, DVDs and books, and to get the low down on their latest work.

Top Celebrity Story One celebrity is selected from them all and put under the spotlight. Plus, a brief interview accompanies the images.

Pec Galleries The nerve centre of Celebpecs! Everyone is sorted into alphabetical order for your perusal. Alternatively, you can search from different organising strategies, like TV Talent, Music Makers, Sports Studs, Black Beauties and Pumped Pecs.

Pec News Entirely ridiculous news stories about men's chests, and more pictures of men's chests.

Pec Shop Products by these men – their workout videos, autobiographies, movies and, heaven help us, albums. For lottery winners only.

The place to get your pec fix.

www.thecruisingground.com
The Cruising Ground

The basic thrust of this site is to tell you about all the cruising areas that exist around the world. Cruising for sex is a much maligned sport, with few loveable or honest participants to guide us. Even George Michael, famously caught at it in LA, burst into tears upon arrest when he could have invited the nice policeman and Channel 9 News to make a flattering documentary of the process. Shame. In London, the headquarters at Hampstead Heath are always busy, and GMFA diligently clean up the mess afterwards during the summertime.

But what about everywhere else? The Cruising Ground covers public parks, toilets, shop loos, motorway service stations and rest areas, squares like Russell Square and Bedford Square, and gives advice on what to expect and what time you're likely to find some action. Messages give further information about what's happening, who's there, whether there are visits or patrols by police officers, park wardens or MI5 operatives, and even when they'll be going. There are hundreds of messages here, and although they mainly focus on well-known places like Finsbury Park, Clapham Common and Holland Walk, there are many surprises, and even people who comment on the state of play in saunas and clubs. Beware of inaccuracies, though, because all this information has come to the site from readers. The site offers books for sale, like Spartacus and Gay London, and there are videos available like Queer As Folk, The Birdcage

overall rating:
★ ★ ★ ★

classification:
sex and lifestyle

updated:
continually

navigation:
★ ★ ★ ★ ★

content:
★ ★ ★ ★

readability:
★ ★ ★

speed:
★ ★ ★ ★ ★

UK

and some porn. You can get on the mailing list too, or read the stories posted about terrible sex experiences, sexual positions and what you got up to last night.

SPECIAL FEATURES

Personals A seemingly unending stream of messages from men all over the world. These take a typically rude form, and usually exclude images.

Advice What happens if you get arrested (outdoor sex is illegal in many places) and have to deal with the police? This section offers advice to those who are resident in the UK on police procedures and your rights. Bear in mind that, although most Metropolitan police officers wouldn't think an arrest for cruising worth the paperwork, they might feel differently if you are in possession of drugs. Also, there is always the planned operation or raid, in which case you could be in a bit of trouble. The advice presented is detailed and accurate.

Escorts A free service to escorts. Enter your details and that's it! Sit back and wait for your new mobile to ring. Most of the guys have linked their intro to their own website with pictures and details.

An interesting and extensive site, and especially worth a look if you're going on holiday.

www.squirt.org
Squirt Cruising Guide

Are you 18 or over? Do you want to cruise with other guys? Then get into this site. This lists cruising areas worldwide, including Australia, New Zealand, Central and South America, Asia, Africa, the Middle East, Europe, the USA and the UK. At the time of review there were over 400 reviews of UK cruising areas, including bathhouses, saunas, beaches, gyms, hotels, nudist groups, parks, toilets, clubs and bars, video arcades and private parties. All the London parks are listed and carry reader comments on the current state of play in these places. I was surprised at the extent of the options, and you can add your own comments to enrich the site further. You can even submit a listing! There's not much advice on this site; unlike the Cruising Ground, it's simply a more brightly coloured site that screams F-U-N. The listings are helpful, and you need to sign up for a membership to get the most out of the site. This only takes seconds. The links to sex sites are good, but expect to pay.

overall rating:
★ ★ ★ ★

classification:
sex and lifestyle

updated:
continually

navigation:
★ ★ ★ ★ ★

content:
★ ★ ★ ★ ★

readability:
★ ★ ★

speed:
★ ★ ★ ★ ★

UK

SPECIAL FEATURES

Squirt Store Dirty DVDs, lube, condoms, leather, lingerie, magazines and toys. What more could a boy want?

A great site to look at before you go on holiday, or if you're tired of your current sexual options and want to try something new.

gay

overall rating: ★ ★ ★ ★	
classification: lifestyle	
updated: daily	
navigation: ★ ★ ★ ★ ★	
content: ★ ★ ★ ★ ★	
readability: ★ ★ ★	
speed: ★ ★ ★ ★ ★	
UK	

www.ukgaydirectory.com
UK Gay Directory

Bright graphics and club music hit you as you click onto this site; you may feel the need to switch the music off fast. This flashy site has internal window systems to help you stay organised. You need this because, as we all know, the last time you went online you were looking for information about digital cameras and you wound up ordering some pine flooring from Scandinavia instead. There are so many links here that it's difficult to cover them all, and within these links are yet more links. Some of the things you can find via this site are West End Guides, an overview of Gay London and Tourist London, an A-Z of London Cinemas and Theatres, an accommodation guide – and that's just on one page about London. The chat room here was in use, unlike on so many sites, and the only truly awful part of this site was the endless exhortations from Webmaster Simon to phone premium rate numbers and pay for porn.

SPECIAL FEATURES

Gay Britain Portal A really comprehensive guide to the UK scene. It might be full of advertising, and it takes a few minutes to load up, but it does list everything you might need, including bars, saunas, escorts, travel and galleries. You need age check for these galleries, but everything else, including all the extensive guides, is free. There are links to just about everything that's relevant, and the site has picked up on lots of mainstream shopping sites as well as those that retail gay-related items.

Travel This is a huge resource, listing hotels, apartments and gay-friendly B&Bs everywhere. There are short descriptions of the place, contact details and links to online booking services.

Shopping What I like about this site is that it links you to Boxman for music, Blackstar for Region Two DVDs (European standard) and Amazon.com for Region Ones (USA and Canada standard). Although US videotapes won't play on UK machines, you can get two-region DVDs here and get a standard UK Region Two DVD player adjusted to play Region One DVDs, though they won't play unless you've had the adjustment made to your UK machine. The site also links to GameWire for computer games. As I observe in the shopping section of this book, before you buy a DVD player, decide whether to get a Region Two player or a multi-region machine. With a multi-region machine you can take advantage of releases all over the world instead of waiting for European manufacturers to bring out what you want in Region Two. The other thing is that the US price is usually about $20 while in the UK it's £20; Mission: Impossible 2 was $10.50 on Amazon.com. Even with US delivery charges, shipping more than three discs from the US works out cheaper, and more titles have been released in the US market. You can get Butterfield 8 in the US but not in the UK.

A flashy, active site that still manages to keep on top of its basic function as a source for information and vital links.

gay

overall rating: ★ ★ ★	
classification: sex	
updated: daily	
navigation: ★ ★ ★ ★ ★	
content: ★ ★ ★ ★	
readability: ★ ★	
speed: ★ ★ ★ ★	
US	

www.xxx-xxx-xxx.com
On-Line Gay Movies

With VHS quality having been much improved in the last five years, and DVD pornography now available, it is difficult for a computer screen using Real Player to compete – and the pornography on here is full of glitches. Although most sites are now encoding in Real Player 8, there is a charge to download this new software. Still, this site is the best and, at $11.95 for two hours, the cheapest of the Real Player sites. There are few special features, just a selection of videos to watch. You can pause and stop them at any time, but bear in mind that if you haven't got a Pentium III and a 56k modem this kind of porn will probably be no good to you.

Choose from a wide range of titles, such as features, series, blowjob, 2 and 4 hour, black, gay, interracial and masturbation. All the films are professionally made and have continuous sex in place of stories; the participants treat each other like shit and it's all a bit realistic for my taste. Check out how RealPlayer works before you spend any money, so that you aren't wasting time when you're meant to be watching. Bear in mind that once the initial charge period has passed, RealPlayer 8 will probably become free too. Click on user info to find out how much time you have left.

A straightforward, inexpensive RealPlayer porn site.

OTHER SITES OF INTEREST

The Number.com
http://www.thenumber.com

You're probably already familiar with the advertising for this, which features a naked man holding up a towel and inviting you to use a chat-line service. Well, there's more to the beautifully designed thenumber.com than that, including columns and features, chat about DNA magazine and reality TV shows with some sharpness and wit, up-to-the-minute online polls and just about everything else you could wish for. The chat room was always empty when I visited this site, and the message boards were very much US based. The Number has its own email service, along with massive links to US shopping sites.

Now UK
http://www.nowuk.net

This initially seemed to be a promising site. The first thing I noticed was that they were selling chart albums for £9.99 (Eminem and Stephen Gately), p&p included. Actually, it turned out that everything for which the site was taking credit was second-hand. Like Axiom, they offer seven-day TV, satellite and radio listings, plus links to the main radio stations, so that, with RealPlayer, you can listen while you surf. But the chat room was a link to gay.com, and so it went on: a second-hand sales message board linked you up to a proper business concerned with second-hand sales, while the SMS messaging service linked you to the Lycos SMS messaging service. However, Now UK are offering free internet access and email accounts. It is also the home of Mr Gay UK. Harry French was 2000's winner, and you can click on the link to see him, read his diary, sign his guestbook and get his stats. Also, there are links to other people's MP3 download sites. Remember, MP3 is a confusing online resource at the moment, generally because you have to pay for most tracks. Also, the quality is questionable and it takes a top-of-the-range computer to achieve glitch-free playback.

SM Gays
http://www.smgays.org

SM Gays is a non-profit-making social and educational group for gay men who are interested in consensual, sexual sadomasochism. They've been meeting since July 1981, and their aim is to encourage safe and lawful SM practices through the sharing of information among people with similar interests. The group is run by volunteers. There's a list of upcoming events, all of which are held at The Hoist (see bars), on the third Thursday of every month, from 8pm to midnight. These offer you

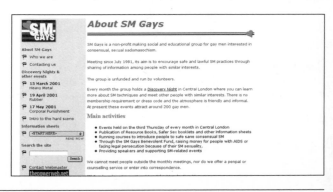

an opportunity to learn about SM sex, model the outfits and perform simple medical procedures without general anaesthetic. SM Gays publishes a number of books and leaflets, and information about all of them is on this site. You'll find information on SM sex and UK law along with a pen-pal service; plus, of course, you can email them with your own ideas, comments or appeals for assistance with those chains he's left you in.

Scene Events.com
http://www.sceneevents.com
This useful site announces itself as 'the world's first online gay accommodation booking service'. You can book hotels and flights to anywhere in the world, and they recommend hotels in Paris, Berlin, Sydney, Sitges and London which are guaranteed to be gay friendly. The site sometimes suffers from technical problems, but you can book over the phone when this happens.

Czech boys.com
http://www.czechboys.com
Heavily advertised in the gay press, this new sex site offers images of Czech boys for your pleasure. Ridiculously young but presumably over 18, the guys selected are from one of the world's most war-torn and poverty stricken nations. The giveaway is that most of them don't look comfortable on camera – they're probably straight and hoping that these web pages will only ever be broadcast in the West so that their mums and dads won't see them! Membership costs $18.95 per month, and gets you the usual live shows, videos, stills and message boards.

Out UK
http://www.outuk.com

You'll find free galleries, a message board, an empty chat room and features on this new UK site. The features are of a high standard, the page design is good, and the news service takes some beating. You'd be better to click on here, frankly, than reading the Pink Paper.

Blue Door
http://www.bluedoorcollection.com

This US site retails some very beautiful postcards, birthday cards and calendars, all featuring images of men. Unfortunately, there's a $16.95 international delivery charge so it's only worth using Blue Door if you have a large order to place. Still, there's nothing in the UK which compares with the unique collection and very high standards, both in terms of models and photography, that you find here.

Adonis
http://www.adonis-art.com

Instead of buying those naff photographs of naked men to send to your friends, you could buy art instead. This site sells drawings and paintings of the male form, some of which are excellent. There are also details of current exhibitions and paintings for sale, since Adonis is a dealership.

Electronic Law Journals Project
http://elj.warwick.ac.uk/jilt/internet/97_1akdz

The regulation of pornography and child pornography on the internet. Scary stuff.

stars

Hooray! When I was a little lad, you could only find out about pop people and film people from Look In, Smash Hits or Just Seventeen. On TV there was Top of the Pops and the fabulously automated The Chart Show, and everything else to do with fandom was going on inside the privacy of your own head. Now, everything that is going on inside everyone's head is now displayed, in the absence of an available television crew, online. Anything to sell ad space and keep those counters ticking over, it would seem, and any old rubbish appears on the net about anyone who has been even remotely touched by fame. In the post-millennium days of Big Brother, celebrity is a somewhat tragic currency, and most of the stuff on the net isn't worth pausing over. Poor journalism and hopeless photography squabble for space with nonsense, lies and spite, while wealthy entertainers try to win control of domain names (like madonna.com) which shrewd entrepreneurs bought in 1826. In the middle of all this crap, the really good sites made by stars or for stars gleam like diamonds. There are sites on everyone who is releasing records, making television or films, and writing books; however, I have chosen to focus on a few of the stars who have been adopted by gay men as their own.

barbra streisand

overall rating: ★ ★ ★	
classification: star site	
updated: continuous	
navigation: ★ ★ ★ ★ ★	
content: ★ ★ ★ ★ ★	
readability: ★ ★ ★	
speed: ★ ★ ★ ★ ★	
US	

www.barbrastreisand.com
Official Streisand Site

When I initially logged onto this site I was convinced it was a spoof. It had to be, but it isn't. When you click on this official site you get Barbra's Truth Alerts. As she puts it: 'Thanks for taking a look at our Truth Alert section. I wanted to tell you why we decided to try a brand new way to tell it like it really is; to nail the lies before they become established as fact.' You almost go along with her reasoning until, inevitably, you have to laugh. This is not 'truth telling' so much as having a go at the journalists who have had a go at Barbra – and this kind of response just gives those journalists more power over her.

The more you enter Barbra-world, the more you suspect that here is a woman trapped in a desperate sense of hurt over the way she has been viewed and dealt with by the world. Her state of mind is practically hanging off the page. Hard done by, vastly talented (unlike most of her competitors) and yet mostly unsung, criticised for her appearance and acting – she must wonder what the hell she has to do to feel free and acceptable. Having a good laugh at yourself would be one thing, but that wouldn't be Barbra, would it? That's partly why she's such a big, long-running star: she's operating out of an entirely different set of myths from Madonna and Cher. The site is fascinating but it's really sad, too. The problem with Truth Alerts and the Truth Archive is that every reader knows that Barbra herself would not tell the truth about certain matters, because she is a very private person. Why should she? It's her life.

SPECIAL FEATURES

Biography 'The career of Barbra Streisand has been paved with bold, creative achievements and highlighted by a series of firsts.' Do you get the psychological picture? I mean, so what if her career is full of bold, creative achievements? So is everyone's! On it goes: 'The Prince of Tides was the first motion picture directed by its female star ever to receive a Best Director nomination...' Ugh. Doesn't she realise she might be better off just singing something?

Statements 'From time to time, Ms Streisand may have statements to make either in response to questions and/or comments made about her, or simply because she feels strongly about a subject and wants to convey her personal sentiment.' From time to time I make statements, too – would you like to hear those?

Charities She's involved, good on her, with Breast Cancer coalitions, Advocates for Youth, Human Rights, and so on. Whatever you might think about stars and charities, and the irony of it all, you have to hand it to her: she works to get stuff done.

Discography When completed, this section will contain lists of everything she has recorded and allow you to hear a sound byte from each track. The output and range of her work is astonishing, and we all know she has an extraordinary voice.

Filmography lists every film in which Barbra has appeared, along with a brief synopsis and credits. The film of hers which sticks in my mind is Nuts, but even in that there are numerous problems of characterisation and story. Obviously

The Prince of Tides and The Mirror Has Two Faces aren't worth watching. Possibly no-one has ever suggested to Barbra that she is not attractive enough to play most of the roles she goes for, but then this goes back to the psychodrama which seems to have dominated her entire life.

TV is an odd little list of everything Barbra has done on TV,

including her Ed Sullivan appearances back in the 1960s. I'm glad there is no list like this with my name on it.

Since this is the 'official' site, it is intriguing, and it gives so much away it's unbelievable. Far from cultivating mystery, the site seems to expose exactly where Ms Streisand is at – and few people would envy her in the slightest.

OTHER BARBRA SITES OF INTEREST

Barbra Streisand
www.barbra-streisand.com

A nicely put together and fresh site blessed with the objectivity the official site lacks. There's a promotion of the new album Timeless – Live in Concert, extensive news, a list to which you can add your name, and listings of tracks and movies. Once again, you can't help thinking that Barbra's best achievements were in the Sixties and Seventies, and that all that therapy has ruined her. All the same, it's hard to convey the madness and excitement of a Streisand concert, much of which is caused by the fact that she hardly ever does one. Forget about the truth alerts and write her a letter telling her to get back on stage.

The Barbra Streisand Music Guide
www.bjsmusic.com

A very informative and detailed site about the star. The description of Barbra's wedding to James Brolin in June 1998 is 1000 words long and really charming. Full information is given about her final concerts in New York on September 27th and 28th 2000, along with extremely detailed information about her recording career, film career and television appearances. This is the site for the diehard fan, and it includes notes on Barbra's whingeing about having 'a thousand frights and fears' when she goes on stage and that she 'doesn't enjoy it', which is why she's not doing it any more. Perhaps it would never occur to her to grit her teeth and just do it, for those of us who have put her in her grand position by buying her records and grimaced through her films? No, it wouldn't. To get Babs to do anything you have to 'love her', whatever that means.

cher

www.cher.com
Official Cher Site

Between the über-commercial megastardom of Madonna and the gay-iconette loveliness of Kylie, Cher stands statesmanlike. Hugely talented, misunderstood, hated for having sex with fit young lads, and yet brilliant on the silver screen, she has withdrawn slightly from the fame game but remains one of the world's very few one-name stars. No-one has yet done Cher justice on the net but, in the meantime, this somewhat formal site suits her. It delivers Cher news and events in a clipped Reuters-like style: Cher will be meeting Bill Clinton tonight. Spin-free writing is such a rarity these days.

SPECIAL FEATURES

Cher News What she's doing. She's at political conferences! She's everywhere! She's giving out awards! Go Cher!

Cher Store Cher wear, jewellery, music, books, household and a sale! Directions to www.cherdirect.com. Hot foot there immediately. It's all so organised; she really has seen you coming and is overcharging magnificently. Go Cher!

Cher Friends Chastity Bono writes about her daughter, while Cher draws attention to her charity of the moment, a craniofacial organisation. Or promotes an LA rock band.

| overall rating: |
| ★ ★ ★ ★ |

| classification: |
| star site |

| updated: |
| continuous |

| navigation: |
| ★ ★ ★ ★ ★ |

| content: |
| ★ ★ ★ ★ ★ |

| readability: |
| ★ ★ ★ |

| speed: |
| ★ ★ ★ ★ ★ |

| US |

Cher Music, Movies and Tour Info, and her books Here's where you can listen to a wide range of tracks in Real Audio, including most of the Believe album. In Movies you can see her in Tea with Mussolini. Check the tour information to find out when and where she's on. If she's not on, and you've seen everything and heard all the records, read The First Time, about when she went on the Ed Sullivan Show with some lesser personages called Elvis and The Beatles. Both now forgotten, clearly. Go Cher!

Cher Gallery Plastic surgeons all over the world owe Cher their fortunes! She looks younger in the 1980s shots than in the 1960s shots! It's a miracle. In fact, she looks a lot younger than her son.

Cher Chat Yes, once you have read the books, seen the films, looked at the pictures and played the CDs until they're beaten and scratched, you can chat about the lady. Please, they ask, do not respond to hateful posts. Now there's a top way to waste an afternoon...

What can I say? It's Cher, man, the undisputed master of the dual career.

OTHER CHER SITES OF INTEREST

Cher City
www.geocities.com/Broadway/4662/
A simple enough site detailing the star's movies, discography and lyrics, plus showing images of her. It is not cool to have a guestbook or a counter any longer, but you can forgive the web author in this case because the site is so pretty, and so Cher.

The Cher Webring
http://nav.webring.yahoo.com/hub?ring=cher&list
Most of the sites on here, as with most web-ring sites, are wholly awful. There is no educational, entertainment or enjoyment value in looking at them, so don't! Properly developed sites have money and time thrown at them until they work. For example, www.madonnamusic.com would cost you about £32,000 to develop if you approached a design company with similar concepts. Web-ring pages suffer because they are designed by individuals who are learning. Fine, but what that means is that on web-ring sites you'll find a mix of the usual internet clichés – guest books, counters, email boxes, poorly scanned images and people who are about to be sued for putting MP3s on the net. These can be fun, because if you catch them before they are shut down you can put an artist's entire catalogue on your computer. For obvious legal reasons I can't recommend such sites to you in this guide, but they do exist and they typically last for about 48 hours. Happy searching. At the time of review there were 54 Cher sites on the web ring, and they were all horrible.

judy garland

overall rating: ★ ★ ★	
classification: star site	
updated: continuous	
navigation: ★ ★ ★ ★ ★	
content: ★ ★ ★ ★ ★	
readability: ★ ★ ★	
speed: ★ ★ ★ ★ ★	
US	

www.judygarland.net
The Judy Garland Showcase

Judy Garland was one of the foremost entertainers of her era, with amazing abilities in singing, acting and dance that almost no-one can match today. While most of her films for MGM seem anachronistic now, a few like The Clock are worth watching, mainly because Judy is permitted simply to act rather than being obliged to constantly break into song; and, of course, The Wizard of Oz has charmed generations of viewers. This site has a simple, flat presentation set against a yellow-brick-road backdrop, but it does feature some surprises, like a collection of vintage magazine articles on Garland. It's a bit of a shock to learn how clearly and brilliantly Louella Parsons wrote in her heyday, and it is difficult to imagine any major star being this relaxed with a journalist these days. The way studios presented their stars to the public is fabulously naïve, and after half an hour on this site you'll be hard pressed to understand how a world like this once existed.

SPECIAL FEATURES

Biography gives a quick review of a life that encompassed breathtaking success, desperate depression and a few dodgy marriages to gay men. Lapses into sentimentality ('June 22, 1969, Judy enters into eternal life') are forgivable.

FAQs is a rather daunting set of questions and answers, covering everything you ever wanted to know about Garland. It's worth trawling through to find out where the original ruby slippers are.

Memorabilia is where you can find photographs relating to every stage of Judy's life, from her first performances as a child to her posh mausoleum in upstate New York.

Fun, sensitive site on the star.

OTHER GARLAND SITES OF INTEREST

Lesion Nation
www.lesion.com/judy
An absolutely tasteless but somehow quite funny site pretending to give Judy's 'views' on life. Also featuring Ella Fitzgerald and Janis Joplin, geddit?

Beyond the Rainbow
www.beyondtherainbow2oz.com/beachtowels
A highly amusing site retailing Wizard of Oz beach towels. For heaven's sake.

Zianet
www.zianet.com/jjohnson/oz.htm
An excellent resource on The Wizard of Oz, with its cool grey design complimented by a mass of detail and links to buy the video, the special box sets, the DVD and so on.

kylie

www.kylie.com
Kylie Minogue

It isn't often that you really have to say a site is beautiful; but, somehow, that is precisely the effect achieved on kylie.com. Everything, from the smooth, partial track downloads promoting Light Years to the glowing photography which changes contrast as you move your mouse over it, shines with white light. It flatters your browser and you can just picture John Logie Baird cumming in his grave. The press release for Kylie's latest album of pop perfection is a precisely judged bit of prose (it's not easy, when Madonna is dropping her records and Eminem is here, to make sure everyone remembers the point of Kylie Minogue), and, as we all know, Light Years dropped on 25/9/00.

SPECIAL FEATURES

News The latest on Kylie's albums and singles, her appearances at the Sydney Olympics and online interviews. Click for the track listing of Light Years and entry to the collector cards competition, and to hear one minute from each of the album tracks in Real Player.

Downloads Great QuickTime movie of Spinning Around, screensavers to snaffle up, audio clips; you name it, it's here. In the press section you can see the magazine covers the lady

overall rating:	★ ★ ★ ★
classification:	EMI promotional
updated:	continuous
navigation:	★ ★ ★ ★ ★
content:	★ ★ ★ ★ ★
readability:	★ ★ ★
speed:	★ ★ ★ ★ ★
UK	

has adorned of late, though it is slightly odd to note that she is on the cover of Boyz while Madonna is doing Vanity Fair. Sexiness packs more punch than sweetness, take note! Even though Kylie always seems to be at number two it does take all sorts to make up a gallery of celebrities. At least Limahl has dropped from view.

Forum A strange intelligence and fun-shaped cool dominates this forum, oddly enough, so it seems that this Madonna/Kylie, sexiness/sweetness, Trade/GAY thing cuts both ways. Madonna's fan base is thick, badly dressed and bland while Kylie's is booted, suited and summoning DVDs and Galaxy Minstrels from Urbanfetch (see shopping). Cue article for the Evening Standard on a Friday. At the time of review, a mad fuss over collector cards was jostling with heartfelt grief over the death of Paula Yates. The internet is so strange, at times.

The place to begin with Miss Minogue.

http://www.kylie.com/kylieultra.html
Kylie Ultra

Stylish site showing Kylie in a post-modern club interior. This is the site that includes the famous Dress Kylie section exposed by Graham Norton on TV. At the time of review the site was looking for 'Kylies' born after 1987 for a new book, and talking about Light Years. But there is more to it than that – just! The site is interesting for its design and frequent updating.

SPECIAL FEATURES

Dress Kylie This inexplicably joyful feature will put paid to any depression you may have been experiencing for days.

Photography Well-presented shots from the Intimate and Live tour in 1998. Kylie is at her absurdly slim and sexless best throughout.

Kylie Diary A message from Kylie telling how happy she is to have moved record companies (after Deconstruction dropped her), and a potted history of the story so far. There's also a selection of interesting backstage photos.

Video Kylie Download some of her biggest hits and watch them in Real Player.

A charming, illustrated site which uses the web in an interesting way and, well, makes you smile.

overall rating:	★ ★ ★ ★
classification:	music site
updated:	continuous
navigation:	★ ★ ★ ★ ★
content:	★ ★ ★ ★ ★
readability:	★ ★ ★
speed:	★ ★ ★ ★ ★
UK	

overall rating:
★ ★ ★ ★
classification:
star fanzine type site
updated:
continuous
navigation:
★ ★ ★ ★ ★
content:
★ ★ ★ ★ ★
readability:
★ ★ ★ ★
speed:
★ ★ ★ ★ ★
UK

www.kylieminogue.co.uk
Shocked

Excellent Shockwave Flash site, with Links to CDNow, Amazon, QXL and so on, for Kylie-related purchases, wallpaper downloads, interview transcripts and a gallery. The standard of photography is very high and the design has a sleek authority which the main fan site is lacking. It offers a Light Years exclusive featuring the official cover art and track listings, listings for Kylie's albums and a searchable database of Kylie's songs. What I liked about this site was the standard of presentation and the courtesy with which Kylie's work, usually classed as throwaway pop, was treated. Downloads, like the video of Spinning Around, seemed to run more smoothly. For once, here's a Kylie site with class!

www.kylie.co.uk
Kylie – Limbo

This text-heavy promotion and discussion site is the Kylie fan site to go for, featuring scheduled chat, links to Amazon to buy Kylie's music, photography, and masses of kyliemation. There is a huge news section telling you about everything Kylie has been doing and her upcoming releases. News is archived and goes back all year. It was up to date when we visited, and even reported on Kylie's midweek (projected) chart position (number two, quelle surprise) for On a Night Like This. There are also links to the DeConstruction, Mushroom and PWL record labels.

SPECIAL FEATURES

Kylie Evidence An enormous resource of Kylie's videos, discography, photographs, audio and wallpaper to download.

The Kylie Files A large selection of transcripts of Kylie magazine interviews; appear here, and it's not only that! Try 'The Constitution of the Gay Icon Within the Context of Popular Music', which is Paul Watson's final year dissertation. This section is amazingly full, recent and well-presented.

Say Hey An interactive chat and message board bubbling over with Kylie messages. It's camp, endless, mindless, sparkly and dynamic. What an inspiration Kylie is to us all.

For die-hard fans who want information overload and have hours to watch crumble away at a computer screen.

overall rating: ★ ★ ★	
classification: music site	
updated: continuous	
navigation: ★ ★ ★ ★ ★	
content: ★ ★ ★ ★ ★	
readability: ★ ★	
speed: ★ ★ ★ ★ ★	
UK	

madonna

overall rating: ★ ★ ★ ★ ★
classification: music site
updated: continuous
navigation: ★ ★ ★ ★ ★
content: ★ ★ ★ ★ ★
readability: ★ ★ ★ ★ ★
speed: ★ ★ ★ ★ ★
US

www.madonnamusic.com
www.wbr.com/madonna
Madonna Music & Warner Bros Music

There are millions of words about lots of stars on the internet now, but perhaps the person who has had the most written about her is Madonna. As well as tolerating her fame-bound life exceptionally well, Madonna still finds time to make the odd single. These sites – www.madonnamusic.com and www.wbr.com/madonna – are her own sites, designed to promote the album, single and DVD Music.

The madonnamusic.com site takes advantage of shockwave flash and media player software and it has the power, typical of Madonna and her team, to make even the best of other websites look dreary and static. At least six things that I had never seen before happened when I logged on to this page, including new ways of making colour and mouse movement interact, and icons which appeared from nowhere as you swept about the screen. On the madonnamusic.com site you can listen to, watch, buy or download the single Music, but when they say 'watch' they mean a trippily distorted graphic equalizer and colour strips that bounce about as the MP3 file comes through the speakers. Beneath this, a layered play/pause/stop keypad awaits your touch. A site like this, which pushes the envelope of current technology, shows how far there is to go. I did all my reviewing on a Pentium III desktop PC with a 56k v.90 modem, and I had a couple of glitches accessing this site because it was so demanding in terms of graphics, sound and downloading. Perhaps Madonna is on commission to BT and Pacific Bell for sales of ISDN lines, which would process everything just fine.

The Warner Bros site is even better. wbr.com/madonna loads up the music single soundtrack and then pulls back the curtains to reveal the lady herself and a selection of sales-orientated buttons. It's amazing to see what a star at the height of her powers can persuade her company to do on her behalf. It's all here, taking full advantage of technology. Warner Brothers have produced another benchmark site which anyone in the industry would appreciate. Other music sites just look horrible by comparison.

SPECIAL FEATURES
Madonnamusic.com features the video and an MP3 download of Music (single). The Warner site features news, track listings and a tour teaser but no downloads.

Fine examples of how the latest technology can be embraced in a site, without being unwieldy and off-putting to the average fan.

overall rating: ★ ★ ★ ★	
classification: madonna	
updated: continuous	
navigation: ★ ★ ★ ★ ★	
content: ★ ★ ★ ★ ★	
readability: ★ ★ ★ ★	
speed: ★ ★ ★ ★ ★	
US	

www.madonnanet.com
Madonna Hub

Want a Madonna net email address? Well, you can get one here. This page is clearly the creation of people who adore her and want you to feel the same. It's original, bright and funny.

SPECIAL FEATURES

Pictures We have all seen Madonna carefully made up and worked over by post-production until she looks lit from within, but fewer fans will have seen her participating in a school play in 1971 – or, indeed, in any of the situations shown in this section, which carries images from her entire life.

Music People all over the world have remixed Madonna's songs, some with her permission and some without. There is even a radio station which plays nothing but her stuff. This is where you can hear it and download it.

Great for its photography of the youthful Maddie.

www.madonnafanclub.com
Madonna's Fan Club, 'Icon'

Not famed for her excessive modesty, Madonna has named her fan club ICON - and this is it. Begin with the message 'Mirwais is the shit...', take the ICON poll, read the giant news archive, or sign up for the ICON magazine, now in its 34th issue.

SPECIAL FEATURES

News A truly vast resource on what's happening with the star, including spinner.com, who are playing her album in a global Net cast, along with news about her relationships, children, films, records and magazine interviews. Since this is coming from the star's 'people', you can be sure that it's accurate and fair. There is, however, an awful lot of it. The Biography is disappointing and, beside the flash sites promoting Music, this one has an unforgivable deadness to it which surprised me.

ICON Magazine A whole magazine devoted to Madonna, which comes as part of membership privileges. You can join the fan club online for $48.

Memorabilia Purchase Madonna items online from the Boy Toy catalogue using the SSL cart service, but beware that every last thing is overpriced!!

Very much an official site, which although slick and glossy, is slightly impersonal.

overall rating:
★ ★ ★ ★

classification:
star fan club

updated:
daily

navigation:
★ ★ ★ ★ ★

content:
★ ★ ★ ★ ★

readability:
★ ★ ★ ★

speed:
★ ★ ★ ★ ★

US	R

overall rating:	★ ★ ★
classification:	music site
updated:	continuous
navigation:	★ ★ ★ ★ ★
content:	★ ★ ★ ★
readability:	★ ★ ★
speed:	★ ★ ★ ★ ★
SWI	

www.sindrismadonnapage.com
Madonna Music

Of all the Madonna pages, this was my personal favourite. Sindris, a Swiss resident, has done her best to settle that leaving-the-house question forever by slinging every Madonna-related item ever produced onto this page. She is in trouble for

making MP3 files of Madonna songs and putting them here for download (imprisonment, heh heh), but you have to love her for being so clueless about international copyright and for mucking about with a heavyweight like Warner Bros. Oh dear. The site opens with Madonna's quote of the week (chosen from all her sayings since fame dawned in 1983) and a bit of news.

SPECIAL FEATURES

News/Gallery/Tour Like most 'news' sections on Madonna, this one is predictably huge, and it was especially so when Music was being released. Revealing snaps of Madonna through the ages are shown in Gallery, while the tour section tries to figure out when the serially pregnant star will next take to the stage.

Discography/Videography/Filmography/Lyrics This is the place to send your phoned friend when you get a Madonna question on Who Wants to be a Millionaire? The page scores by allowing you to print out stills from Maddie's videos, which often prove moodier and more artistic than the videos themselves, and read the biography of each particular promo's director. The discography shows obscure imports, the singles from the album and the production credits, while you can print out the lyrics from any Madonna song (Madonna Fact # 10,906: she has released a song for every letter of the alphabet bar Q, U, X and Z.)

Interviews Did you miss Madonna mouthing off about music, dancing, Sean Penn, Woody Allen, the Pope or houses in London? A selection of the best interviews from the years are here, though clearly some houses like Conde Nast have refused copyright permission. It's hardly surprising, either; Vanity Fair still sell out back issues that have Madonna interviews in. Well presented and easy to print, and including, for example, the mouthy tart's words in The Face about Music, her 'love you but fuck you' record.

Magazine Covers Madonna's face is a relentless magazine-shifter and her chameleon-like image, which somehow resembles everyone you've ever met, shows up on about seven magazines around the world each month. It has done for years, so do the maths. Sindris has, and she has compiled a feature which even Madonna's staff could consult to see if it's time she did Automart and the East Anglian Fishing Times... oh, someone's saying she did them in 1985. The eerie aspect of this site is that she looks American on the American magazines, German on the German magazines and Spanish on the Spanish magazines. Weird.

A great site which should satisfy even the hungriest of fans.

OTHER SITES OF INTEREST

eil.com
www.eil.com

Massive collection of Madonna memorabilia offered for sale in sterling and US dollars. Just type in Madonna in the artist search engine.

Madonnaweb
www.madonnaweb.com

A cool site, full of Madonna news and web chats with her dancers. It's currently being upgraded and partly under construction. The Madonna Web forum offers the chance to create an account and chat or post messages with other users who are interested in Madonna or related matters.

Fosbrook Online
www.fosbrook.demon.co.uk/madonna-discography-uk.htm

Excellent UK site showing the performance of every one of Madonna's records to date in the UK market.

robbie williams

overall rating: ★ ★ ★
classification: star site
updated: continuous
navigation: ★ ★ ★ ★ ★
content: ★ ★ ★ ★ ★
readability: ★ ★
speed: ★ ★ ★ ★ ★
UK

www.robbiewilliams.com
Official Robbie Site

The last surviving member of Take That goes from strength to strength, though it's not easy to see why. Whenever you see him on TV he's moaning about not breaking America, which sounds rather ungrateful, or lording it over members of his old pop group. Anyone can see that luck and marketing play a bigger role than talent in determining who went the distance. The internet holds many pages which consist of paeans of praise to the boy; this is the official site, set in black and grey.

SPECIAL FEATURES

Chat Room Talk about Robbie until your fingers ache. This proved to be one of the busiest chat rooms I found online, but nobody was talking about sex, just about... Robbie Williams.

Music Watch tour footage of Robbie with Real Player.

Inner Sanctum The inner sanctum shows you how to become a member of the fan club and allows you to read Robbie's E-Diary. It also appears to cause lots of info-boxes to pop up telling you where Robbie will be playing next and how to get tickets.

The official page.

the spice girls

www.c3.vmg.co.uk/spicegirls
Official Virgin Spice Girls Site

This is the official Virgin Records Spice Girls site, and therefore the only site allowed to play you the new single Let Love Lead the Way and show you the video. It's a well-designed site, featuring links to the girls' own sites, web chats, a making-of-video for the new single, and a choice of file sizes so that you can choose how long you want to spend hooked up to the net downloading. Sound is presented via Real Player, which brings its own problems of sound and net congestion, something we must all learn to live with when attempting to access global

overall rating: ★★★★
classification: star site
updated: continuous
navigation: ★★★★★
content: ★★★★★
readability: ★★★
speed: ★★★★★
UK

phenomena such as the Spices. Video comes through QuickTime, which is a more reliable format. It's worth watching the video just to see how much work goes into these promotional products: more than 300 separate shots are edited together, each of which must have required hours of set up, lighting and post-production, and the girls all look magically beautiful. Considering how ordinary they are, the production is miraculous. The salmon-pink site is bright, well designed and endlessly interactive: if you miss something it will be referred to 10 more times in other locations on the site. You can join the email list for news and gossip, join the fan club and receive Insider Spice, the magazine, or sit back and view the Spice Girls' special video welcome. When you're done with that, buy tour merchandise.

SPECIAL FEATURES

Web Chats Throughout October 2000, the four girls gave web-chat interviews on this site, finishing with Victoria on 23 October 2000. In these, they answered a selection of questions posted by readers via email from all over the world. These make for typically exuberant interviews; they don't tell you an awful lot about who these four women really are, but they're a laugh nonetheless.

News This section leads you to the Spice Girls' individual pages. Melanie B is at http://c3.vmg.co.uk/melanieb; Melanie C is at www.northern-star.co.uk; and the others have yet to present theirs. These links are combined with brief interviews which capture the girls as they are all collaborating on a new album, releasing a book called Forever Spice and doing solo projects which include albums, shows and films. Do they ever stop?

Competition The site has been giving away articles of Victoria's clothing every day. Each is emblazoned with a suitable slogan like 'I hate shopping' or 'I love Becks'. Underwear does not appear to be available.

Planet Spice Send an email card to your friends or boss or just to BT, they'll love it.

C3 C3 is the Virgin Records site for all its artists, including Martine McCutcheon, Tomcat and Billie. Follow the links!

A cheeky, chirpy site with a great design and perfect copies of the new Spice video for you to download and play while you do your online banking.

OTHER SPICE SITES OF INTEREST

Northern Star
www.northern-star.co.uk
Melanie C's site has a kicking design, sound clips, tour info, pictures and interviews. She alternates between looking cheeky and sexy, and makes chirpy contributions. She looks like Madonna in them, but I've always liked her videos. You can see them in full on this site. Check out I Turn to You, from Northern Star. Lovely.

Melanie B
www.melanie-b.com
Great design on this solo site from Melanie B, also touring with her own material and a solo album. QuickTime interviews and great photography hint that this Spice Girl might have more tricks up her sleeve than the others. A watch-this-space site.

Geri Halliwell
www.geri-halliwell.com
Official site of the ex-Spice Girl, featuring music, video, biography, photos and news.

Halliwell Heaven
www.gerihalliwell.co.uk
Unofficial site with loads of information on Geri, photo galleries, links and news.

Spice Shack
www.musicfanclubs.org/spiceshack
Download songs and lyrics.

Spice Girls Photo Gallery
www.spicepix.com
Images of the girls.

Steve McGarry's Spice Girls Cartoon Strip
www.stevemcgarry.com/archive/SpiceGirls.asp
Cartoons from Steve McGarry's homepage.

Emma Bunton Unofficial Fan Club
www.emma-bunton.com

emmabunton.co.uk
www.emmabunton.co.uk
Unofficial shrines to Emma Bunton.

Victoria: Goddess of Spice
www.geocities.com/SunsetStrip/Palladium/5167
Tribute to Victoria featuring photographs, biography and links.

bars and clubs

I think my peak experience as I was preparing this guide was the moment when I had my www.gay.com window open (with my picture there for the eyes of the world to see), my Big Brother RealPlayer camera going, my Amazon order going through, my Tesco order going through, my Organics Direct order going through, my www.stanleyacropolis.com casino Blackjack box open waiting for my credit card to be authorised, my calculator comparing Viagra prices around the world and my www.updates.com page telling me what new files my computer needed. At the same time, I had my Word window open, in which I was penning a review, Outlook Express scanning for emails, a virus program protecting me from nasty unwanted files and my CD player spinning Ministry sounds from Ibiza. I think I was also paying the phone bill at www.abbeynational.com. God, I suddenly thought, haven't we come a long, long way from the days of ZX Spectrums with their nasty silver printer paper (two inches wide, as I recall; what was the point?) and the BBC Micro with its unfathomable programming language? The internet now resembles an infinite world in which anything is possible as long as someone, somewhere has the idea and the money to present it to you effectively. Clearly the next step in computer technology is going to be a much larger screen where all your open windows don't overlap, perhaps a four-foot-square, wraparound item that can show everything you need clearly and in real time. Coming to a copy of T3 near you.

When it comes to bars and clubs, the developments have been no less breathtaking. With their chat rooms, feedback forms, queue-jumping flyers, images of wasted customers, shops, histories, promotions and DJ information, some of them are far better than the clubs they advertise. And, since you are in your own home, you can be confident that a gin and tonic will cost you 50p instead of four quid. What's more, you'll be able to happily have a wee in a clean toilet, and you won't have to risk your life and liberty transporting yourself, your catch and your pills home in a mini-cab ride at dawn through London. Why didn't we think of this earlier? I can confidently predict that in 10 years' time a club, in order to attract custom, will have to be equipped so brilliantly that it could stage the Olympic Games at the drop of a hat. Good news then: no more vibrating dance floors, substandard DJs and rude bouncers, or the club will last a week at best.

overall rating:	★ ★ ★
classification:	club
updated:	none
navigation:	★ ★ ★ ★ ★
content:	★ ★ ★ ★ ★
readability:	★
speed:	★ ★ ★ ★ ★
UK	

www.crashlondon.co.uk
Crash

Crash has a sexy black and red website with photographs of the club in action, reports on upcoming events and biogs of the DJs who play there. The photography brilliantly conjures up the sense of hopeless confusion that is the key experience sought out every Saturday by these shirtless Vauxhall clubbers. I don't know exactly why but this page makes you want to go clubbing more than all the others. Scratchy music opens the site, and then the graphics take you on a giddy virtual ride. The site is a bit new and the merchandise is not available yet, but the chat room was surprisingly busy with people asking what the backroom action was like – I've never seen a backroom at Crash – and how much it costs to get in. Gripping stuff. Of course, there's no substitute for a real session at Crash. But if you require a mild, midweek collision, this site should do you the power of good. Join the mailing list to keep in touch.

A snazzy stop for your virtual Crash fix.

www.dtpm.net
DTPM

An unashamedly drug-fuelled, interstellar space mission, housed in a Shockwave Flash casing, is what the DTPM team have prepared for you. You can feast your eyes on it whenever it happens not to be a Sunday. In spite of brilliant design, however, there isn't a single sound on this site – maybe they just wanted to reproduce the silence of space as well, in which case it's a sterling achievement. View moody photographs of the Fabric rooms, empty and looking unusually clean, click on the photo of the month for the latest image of a space cadet mid-mission, or read the nicely presented DJ profiles. The Fiction promotion is cool, and it features one of those irritating online games that you play for 40 seconds and then retire from, defeated and bored. I loved it.

SPECIAL FEATURES

History You already knew that DTPM began life in 1993 in a restaurant called Villa Stefano in Holborn, London. Opening at noon and closing at 8pm, it popularised Sunday afternoon clubbing, catering for those who hadn't been to bed since 1975. Then it was Bar Rumba, then The End (and open until 4am), and now Fabric. And to think it all began with just one table and a Walkman connected up to Dixons travel speakers in Villa Stefano, so many years ago. From tiny acorns, indeed.

overall rating:
★ ★ ★

classification:
club

updated:
none

navigation:
★ ★ ★ ★ ★

content:
★ ★ ★ ★ ★

readability:
★ ★

speed:
★ ★ ★ ★ ★

UK

overall rating: ★ ★ ★	
classification: club	
updated: none	
navigation: ★ ★ ★ ★ ★	
content: ★ ★ ★ ★ ★	
readability: ★ ★	
speed: ★ ★ ★ ★ ★	
UK 🔒	

www.fridge.co.uk
The Fridge

Opening with music and light, the Fridge site packs a deafening punch if you arrive unprepared, speakers set to normal CD levels. The site offers the usual message boards (we love the Fridge, yeaahh!), mailing lists and news, but at the time of review the DJ samples weren't operating. The music guide is a bit repetitive; they keep saying they are doing 'uplifting' this and 'uplifting' that, as if there were a melancholy, depressing alternative that anyone would risk in a night club. The blue and orange site design seems oddly suited to the place. Perhaps it's because, while you wouldn't call the Fridge cutting edge, it does have a realness and charm that a more calculated venue like Fabric lacks. It's the same with the site. You won't be gawping at stunning graphics, but then you won't be yawning either.

The site doesn't completely work; for instance, it doesn't make you pine for the weekend as other sites will. Indeed, the long queues outside the real-world place offer a much stronger advertisement for what's going on inside than this site, or the unchanging, waxed male images that have been slapped on Fridge flyers for years. Whether you love or hate the music, the Fridge remains one of the best places to people-watch, either from the balcony, snuggled in those old theatre benches gazing down at the crowd below or checking out the men sliding through the aisle in the café. The Galleries offer a glimpse of the interior, with customers looking typically wasted and joyful as they fast approach their five o'clock coma.

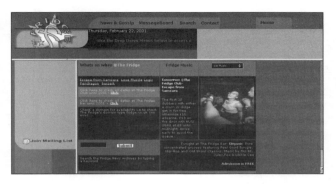

History This is the strongest aspect of the site, featuring a Time Out journalist's take on the development of The Fridge over the years, Andrew Czezowski's imprisonment for tax evasion and the strange declaration that he and Susan Carrington 'now pay half a million pounds a year in tax'. Do we need to know this? It's clearly been a struggle, and most people know that the club has launched many a night which had to be withdrawn shortly thereafter. The only night anyone needs to visit the Fridge is Saturday, when the place heaves with muscle boys and people who are willing to pay to watch them, the upstairs loo is driven over its fire occupancy limit (why can't these boys queue outside?), and everyone revs up for parties, shagging or Trade.

Where are we? Not a question about the club's development but something better: a sexy map drawn on an overhead photo of downtown Brixton. Worth seeing, if only to note how Victorian London still appears from above. It really does look millions of years old here. Major places are shown including the Ritzy, Dogstar and the Town Hall. Pity they didn't add a police car screaming down Coldharbour Lane to make another 'arrest'.

Merchandise Currently just the Samara CD on sale. Surely everyone is desperate for a Fridge pen and pencil set? Betcha can't wait.

The Fridge Bar Spin offs can beat the originals in some respects, and the Fridge Bar is the best place in Brixton to meet for a late or quick drink. You can lose yourself in the basement if you want to dance. This link is useful because it tells you what's going on every night at the bar and what kind of music you can expect, so you won't turn up in your white stilettos expecting Blondie.

Not quite as sexy and seductive as it ought to be, but still, a fair match for the much-loved club.

www.g-a-y.co.uk
Gay Club Promotion Site

Bright red things and bright yellow things and bright blue things are just exactly what you'd expect from that most subtle of night spaces, G.A.Y. The first thing you're told about is what's on tonight and, like everything on this site, it's all done in loads of different colours and really brill typefaces! Yeah! Basic club information and pretty maps jostle with opportunities for you to sign up as a member (for undisclosed benefits) and ads for the G.A.Y. albums, future nights, and such like.

SPECIAL FEATURES

Unusually, the G.A.Y. site offers information about where to stay in London if you are visiting from out of town. You can even book a room online. Jeremy Joseph doesn't miss a trick, does he? What next, a loyalty card?

Yeah! Brill! G.A.Y.! Cheesy as you like, and nothing more or less than what you expect.

overall rating:	★ ★
classification:	club
updated:	weekly
navigation:	★ ★ ★ ★ ★
content:	★ ★ ★ ★ ★
readability:	★ ★
speed:	★ ★ ★ ★ ★
UK	

overall rating: ★ ★ ★
classification: club
updated: weekly
navigation: ★
content: ★ ★ ★ ★
readability: ★ ★
speed: ★ ★ ★ ★ ★
UK 🔒

www.heaven-london.com
Heaven Nightclub

Excellent black and grey graphics assault the eye as the Heaven page loads. Heaven was one of the first genuine dance clubs in London, opening in 1979 and owned for a time by Richard Branson. We all know that it pioneered the idea of different dance floors playing different sounds (they didn't even think of this at Studio 54), offering diverting live shows, beer specials, horny boys and a cruising balcony from which customers can select their targets.

So, does the website give you a feel for the club? Well, there aren't any queues, which contrasts rather with the actual place (though if you can't blag your way past the doorman you need to adjust your gaydar), and it does go over the top (Wayne G is a 'superstar DJ'?). Even so, it somehow makes you feel like you are lost in the blackness of the main floor, and that anything would be possible if you could just get your hands on a couple of extra pills. As with so many of the better-designed sites these days, Heaven has taken advantage of the fast-loading Shockwave Flash animation software, giving the site a cutting-edge look. There are links to other trendy, must-be-seen places, too. As with the G.A.Y. site, you can print out a web voucher online which gives you cheaper entry (and unlike the vouchers in magazines, you can print out more copies online and hand them out to everyone). The main problem with this site is navigation. I conducted my research by using Internet Explorer 5 to visit sites on five separate occasions over a month; each time, I found that the Heaven site failed to load properly, and that the back and forward buttons on the browser didn't work. Sort it out, lads!

SPECIAL FEATURES

What's On Saturday is Heaven, as if we didn't know, with 'Superstar' DJ Wayne G on the main floor, all kinds of mad people presiding over the Star Bar, and soul and rare grooves in the Dakota Bar. The crowd, we are told, is 'gay'. Fruit Machine is on Wednesdays and suits the employment-starved partier, or anyone whose boss has no problem with sleeping employees. Here we find that matchless institution known as the Powder Room (every possible double meaning intended – why don't they shoot a Persil commercial there?), along with Urban FM in the Dakota Bar. There's information on pricing, dress code (none), opening times and location. Don't forget the new Monday nighter, Popcorn, and the straight night, There, on Fridays.

News Not headline news but Heaven news, of course, which is far more interesting than what's happening in the Middle East. Heaven is débuting in Ibiza at Amnesia. Congratulations to Matthew from Woking, who won a trip to the fabulous island! You can join the mailing list or follow the link to www.lastminute.com, who sell Heaven tickets in their VIP section. Click news to find out which DJs are still coherent and maintaining the industry-standard intake of spliff.

Venue A lovely little diagram of the club, of which any 10-year-old art student would be proud. See how it all fits together. We all know that Heaven had a costly refurbishment in 1998, that the management freak if a light bulb fails or a dancer hasn't got clean undies on, and they are justifiably proud of their standards. Remember, however, that, as my friend Justin found out last week, spending millions on a place isn't enough to stop other customers throwing up on your Calvin Klein shirt. Yuk.

Shop This is a fairly decent, secure shopping feature, and there is an image of a boy who you can click on to find vests, jackets, caps and the like. I longed for the browse/dress-me option found in the movie Clueless, or something in keeping with the magnetic man on my fridge. The site also has a little swipe at the Stagecoach bus company, asking for a boycott of it. I go everywhere by limousine, don't you?

A lovely taste of the Heaven nightclub. The only thing missing is the sarnie shop.

www.popstarznightclub.com
Popstarz promotional Site

overall rating:	★ ★ ★
classification:	club
updated:	monthly
navigation:	★ ★ ★ ★ ★
content:	★ ★ ★ ★ ★
readability:	★ ★ ★
speed:	★ ★ ★ ★ ★
UK	

Before you do anything else, examine the intriguing Popstarz philosophies: 'Lager – Down it! Dancefloor – Get down on it!! Atmosphere – Ain't no down about it!!!' Socrates would have been proud. Well, you can forgive the grammar because Popstarz is all about not being full of attitude, not taking homosexuality very seriously and being, or at least pretending to be, young. This site, with its blue print set against a sky of stars, is simple and designed to give information. Previous and upcoming nights are reported with exuberance, and it seems a shame that the counter suggested that only 4,000 readers have clicked onto this site. Not only does it make you remember how madly entertaining a nightclub can be, it makes you want to open one yourself. Popstarz reminds us that humans have only as yet scratched the surface of the world of the night, and there are so many permutations that are yet to be tried.

SPECIAL FEATURES

Flyer Once again, you can print out your discount flyer in full colour and get into the place for a mere 20 shillings or thereabouts.

Music Rules Expect to hear indie tunes, alternative tunes, guitar pop, rock, 1970s and 1980s anthems, and such like. Do not expect to hear naff techno, naff house, naff garage, naff boy bands, naff pop and naff Euro. This list would leave most DJs

scratching their heads and thinking that the only thing they have left to play is a blank tape. How satisfying it all is. Send them your request.

A smart and energised site that simply makes you insist on going out.

www.tradeuk.net
Trade Promotions

overall rating: ★ ★ ★	
classification: club promotion site	
updated: weekly	
navigation: ★ ★ ★ ★ ★	
content: ★ ★ ★ ★ ★	
readability: ★ ★	
speed: ★ ★ ★ ★ ★	
UK 🔒	

When Abe Lincoln was in charge of the brand new USA, any member of the public could walk in off the street and give his view on any matter; there was no security. He sat and chatted to you between memos and it took news four months to cross the Atlantic. You'd never guess it could have been like this, would you, from looking at the modern Presidential elections? Likewise with a wee club called Trade, which used to be a sweaty room with turntables and innocent persons lit up with a new drug called Ecstasy which was meant to change the world. Heaven had closed at three in the morning, there was nowhere to go (Russell Square in the rain? No thanks), and you hadn't picked up yet. Then someone got a 24-hour music and dance licence and now more or less the same people are running a global phenomenon. Behind his black shades, I bet Laurence Malice still doesn't know how he did it.

At the modern Trade club in London, which retains its jet-lagged opening hours (it opens when normal entertainment hours are in force in, er, Los Angeles), there are usually three dance floors, a chill-out room, quick and smiley service on coats, drinks and, well, you know what, though it's all a bit low-key post-raid. The DJ booth is like the interior of a Gulfstream jet, the visuals owe more to Industrial Light and Magic than the weak flashes of laser in the beginning, and the only thing they haven't got round to sorting out is the loo. Considering what a cultural thing Trade is,

the website could be far more self-indulgent (as is the horrendously vain offering from The Ministry of Sound), but it isn't. It's simple and sleek. The introduction briefly explains what Trade has accomplished, leaving aside the casualties: hosting the Manumission backroom and touring Australia, America, South Africa, Ireland, Russia and Japan. The residencies in Paris, Scotland and Manchester continue. Record label products break into three categories, which are Trade-lite, medium and full strength. Respect the Trade Collective, they say. A ticker-tape announcement box tells you about Trade birthday parties, while buttons direct you to lists of DJ line-ups on the night, in the main floor and lite lounge, before moving swiftly on to tour details. Images of the place in action shine in rapid sequences from the top right, and the page is cleverly underlaid with fragments of Trade's perfect, out-of-focus advertising. This feature calls to mind those random glimpses which, sadly, are all the memories you have left after a mad night out. You can watch movies of the Love Parade on your Windows Media Player or view the charming interview footage with Laurence and George. The competition is slight (five guest tickets? You mean some people pay to get in?) but at least it's there. The website deals admirably with issues like its membership, messy door policies, famous queues, drug dealers, raids and guest lists by paying no attention to them at all.

SPECIAL FEATURES

DJs Biographies stop short of fawning and instead outline the career path of the person in question. Their remix work is catalogued and their own comments on the club feature prominently. Steve Thomas's claim that 'there is no attitude at Trade' seems a tad unlikely, but I guess we all see what we want to see.

History 'Trade is famous for many things', says the copy. If you need a website to clue you in you're already much, much too late. Everyone knows that Laurence Malice started Trade 10 years ago, everyone knows it's his masterpiece, everyone wants a gold membership, everyone lies about how many times they've been there, everyone wants that guy who's on the second left by the dance floor, and everyone has a story about what they did with whom in the brutal darkness at that post-Pride party back in... now when was it? Perfection.

Shut down your computer and go.

overall rating: ★ ★ ★
classification: club
updated: monthly
navigation: ★ ★ ★ ★ ★
content: ★ ★ ★ ★ ★
readability: ★ ★
speed: ★ ★ ★ ★ ★
UK

www.wildfruit.co.uk
Wild Fruit

Back when you were just three, darling, there was a club that opened in Brighton called Club Shame. Even Flesh in Manchester and Trade in London were two years away from existing in them days. It's all preserved on the magical Wildfruit website, which I found to be the most fun of all the online clubs. The Trade one is (hands up if you're surprised) deadly serious, as if jumping up and down on drugs to music were important or something, while others are weedy and self-conscious. Contrary to these, Wildfruit is a winner: a blast of music to put you in the mood to surf, plenty of pictures of shrewdly lit boys, flyers and photos from the old days, and information on all the current nights. Nowadays Wildfruit takes place at the 1550 capacity Paradox Club, monthly on Mondays, and the site also fills you in on Kinky Booty (Fridays @ Honey Club) and Sundae Sunday.

SPECIAL FEATURES

History Sob with nostalgia as you re-live the bygone age of Club Shame, Subterfuge and Transformer. It's hard to remember any of it clearly, especially the more mystifying facts like the way you used to have Goth clubs, punk clubs and rockabilly clubs, and when, if the music was all right, it was termed 'high-energy'. This was before Ibiza, ketamine, Smirnoff Ice and Ministry of Sound double CDs, if you please: a time when everyone thought that one pair of Nike trainers was enough. Cigarettes were £1.90. It's a wonder that anyone survived.

Q-jump list and online tickets As the website tells you, you can buy tickets from Sell Out Ticketing on 0870 6060204 (it's the UK's only gay and lesbian ticket agency, you know) or get them online, via www.shoppingsweetie.com. Charge me, sweetie. If you send them an email, they'll give you priority and discounted entry to Kinky Booty and Wild Fruit. Get on with it but be discreet; we don't want everyone doing it.

Gallery Be honest with yourself: you need to see thumbnail images of the go-go boys from Wildfruit, don't you? Here's where they are, along with images of the performers and customers over the years. There do seem to be a lot of pictures of Evette – can't think why that is.

Cool club site with music, boys and glitter.

OTHER SITES OF INTEREST

Coco Latte

www.cocolatte.net

It's only a little club, and Atelier is even littler, but it is cool and worth a visit – plus, they do Moët for £20 a bottle. Coco Latte has been on a boat for the summer and that's not been a lot of fun; shortly, it will be at home once more in Mayfair, where it belongs. Links, maps and a sweet design tell you everything that you need to know.

Spyker Demon

www.spyker.demon.co.uk/attitude.htm

One quick page tells you everything that you need to know about another of those upmarket sex landmarks in London.

Central Station

www.centralstation.co.uk

A message greets you: 'We are in the process of bringing you an updated, revised and even better website, with lots of new connections to other sites of interest. We are aware that this site has been a bit static for a little time – sorry about that. We'll try to ensure that we have changes and improvements for you at least once a week from now on so that you know what's going on and what we've got planned.' So, watch that space.

Ku Bar

www.ku-bar.co.uk

Lots of fun graphics and child-drawn images make this site garishly attractive. The introduction takes the form of what's going on right now, and there are plenty of pictures of gay men

standing around in the Ku Bar exuding fear and apathy. Yes! The bar is clearly a success! There's also information about gay tea dances, Mr Gay UK heats to avoid, an email link and a map showing you how to get to the bar. You even get a message centre called In Touch, where you can try to contact people you were too dizzy, afraid or drugged up to approach at the time. And so we have people saying: 'Shane, where did you go, you said you were only going to the loo? I am still hard and waiting for you in Denim, please page me.' And so on. It's all very dispiriting, dubious and completely gay.

The Sauna Bar

www.thesaunabar.com

The Covent Garden Sauna Bar is a cool place and generally cleaner than its competitors, if not quite so free of tedious attitude. They serve fresh fruit juices and vegetable health drinks at Detox on Sundays, and you can also buy alcohol there.

Facilities include a 30 Man Spa, 20 Man Sauna, Steam Room, Bar, Lounge and five rest rooms, and there are masseurs on the premises. There is a gallery showing the interior but no images of overheated males. The site is so squeaky clean that it comes across like a Butlins brochure, and you don't get a feel for how raunchy a decent sauna can be. Sadly, of course, there isn't anything in the UK comparable to the Amsterdam Thermos day and night saunas, and the sauna websites reflect this lack. Begin the campaign now, that's what I say. Perhaps it would be a suitable business venture for Mr Brian Souter?

Tube Club
www.tube-club.co.uk
I still resent the Tube Club for not being Substation, because when I first came to London it was that crowded sweat box which introduced me to sex, drugs and Six New Things To Do In A Toilet that were never mentioned on Blue Peter. You can immediately see that the designers have been influenced by the G.A.Y. page (Jeremy Joseph as a market leader? Heaven help us.), but this doesn't quite cut it in the same bright, bouncy way. There's information here on the Babe and Wig Out nights (remember how you used to dance to Abba and fancy Lionel Richie? Er, no.) and Sunday's private members club, Fevah. You can give feedback, move to the fevah.co.uk page, enter the competitions and take advantage of the monthly offer.

Goose and Carrot
www.gooseandcarrot.co.uk
The Goose and Carrot is one of Croydon's friendliest and most well-known gay pubs. The site is slow-loading, even with a 56k

modem, but it has an innocence about it which is refreshing compared with the hard-sell seriousness of Trade and The Ministry. Details of disco, cabaret and karaoke nights, along with their emails address and real world address, can be found on the pub page. The Galleries are quite fun; pictures taken with tourist flash cameras show the staff and customers, who look a bit less ferocious than those at Rupert Street. Some of them even sport actual smiles. There's also a chat room in the style of Gay.com, but every time I went no-one was on it.

The Hoist
www.thehoist.co.uk
Opening with a startling shot of Mr Hoist 2000, the Hoist site displays 'evidence' of what has been going on inside – a nice touch. This straightforward site tells you where the club is, when it's on, what the dress code is (fairly strict), and what's coming up next.

Skinner's Arms
www.skinnersarms.co.uk
The Skinners Arms styles itself as 'the premier gay venue for Kennington and Camberwell'. Well, the competition is not that ferocious, is it? Still, the fizzing little boxes they have put your information into are interesting, and the links are fun. This was the only site I found which had chosen to place links to QX and Big Brother on there, which was a nice touch. Launched in July, the site has plenty of potential and the fair number of happy, smiling faces in the galleries suggests that the provincial feel of the place somehow works. It takes all sorts. You get the impression that the management put every picture they've

taken online, so if you go there, expect to be seen by everyone. Big Brother is watching you.

Fist
www.ainexus.com/fist
A slightly frightening website, it must be said, all done in black like the club itself. On this site, Miss Suzy Krueger (her real name?) clues a fascinated world into the merits of her so-called 'Fist' establishment; which, fortunately enough, is located quite close to King's College Hospital Accident and Emergency Unit, in case anything should go amiss in that darkroom. Links to other pages include those mysterious shops (see shopping guide) where proper fisting equipment and sundry accessories may be obtained, guides to when the next sphincter-bruising marathon is to take place, and a lot of strange moving arms. Yikes.

Boots Bar
www.bootsbar.freeserve.co.uk
Cruise bar in Birmingham's gay village, and the best bar site of the Birmingham bars. Leave a message in the darkroom.

Clapham Common
www.claphamcommon.co.uk
I'm kidding.

shopping

People used to ask, what can you buy online? Now they wonder what possible product might remain unavailable to a determined shopper with a credit card and a mouse. A private jet? No, you can register for one at www.gulfstream.com (see below for leasing information). In fact, you can buy anything on line now: gear from Harrods, a Fortnums hamper to send to the other side of the world, theatre tickets, a pizza and a new mobile phone.

In presenting a shopping guide geared to gay men, however, we've attempted to draw your attention towards certain 'typical' purchases, as well as remind you about the more fabulous shopping sites that now exist. There is no reason, of course, why a gay person would be drawn to a shopping experience that's any different from that of a heterosexual. If you want excellent food, you're just as likely to go to www.organicsdirect.com as a housewife in Aberdeen, and if you want a book, you'll probably end up at www.amazon.co.uk like everyone else.

Nevertheless, it is not, predominantly, this writer's straight mates who are asking where they can get Viagra online; it is not my parents who are telling me, down the pub, where to get discounted protein drinks; and it is not anyone at all, other than gay men, who are going on about fashion, restaurants, outrageous gifts, last minute flight deals, pornography, eerie music for their MP3 players and made-to-measure, faux-Scottish kilts. So, shop on, honey: all you need is credit.

www.iwantoneofthose.com
Executive Toys

This is one of my favourite sites on the web, for the beauty of its design (by 2am) and the products on offer. Empty consumerism doesn't usually come with the piss already taken out of it and, as the site says, 'this is stuff you don't need but you just really, really want.' What are the products? The site's character, a suited/booted office female, says: 'People often ask me – how DO you define executive products? Well, frankly, my people do that for me... if it looks good and feels good, I want it, and they get it!'

The product range is very seductive: stuff you really won't have seen before and stuff that is so outlandish (like a fighter jet, though I know you've already got one) that you'll wonder if they really mean it. Well, they do! And they deliver in 24 hours. If you don't have the cash to shop just now you can create a wish list and come back when you've saved up or lied through your teeth for another credit card. The minutes pass so pleasantly as you study the top five, wishing someone would buy you gift vouchers... you may never leave. Be careful what you click for. Never mind, this site works as well for dreamers as for purchasers and there are loads of items under £25 that everyone can afford. Spend over £100 and join Club 100 for 10 per cent off everything. Gay men are so appallingly cash-rich that they have a habit of owning everything that is currently for sale. You can never normally think of exciting gifts for them but now, with iwantoneofthose, you can.

overall rating:	★ ★ ★ ★ ★
classification:	shopping
updated:	continuous
navigation:	★ ★ ★ ★ ★
content:	★ ★ ★ ★ ★
readability:	★ ★ ★ ★ ★
speed:	★ ★ ★ ★ ★
UK 🔒	

SPECIAL FEATURES

Executive Cufflinks, walkie talkies, catamarans, ex-BT phone boxes, fibreglass post boxes, NASA pens, cool stationery and other mental things.

Toys and Games Microscooters, roulette sets, mad yo-yos, remote control cars, water pistols, crossbows and kites. Banish boredom forever.

Lifestyle Flame thrower lighters, talking bags, glasses made out of ice, £1,000 coffee machines, cool fridges. Irresistible.

Want one? Course you do. The place to come when you've decided to give up trying to distinguish between what you want and what you need.

www.gulfstream.com
Gulfstream Aerospace Corporation

Ever dreamed of owning a private jet? Well, you can get one second-hand, as this site happily points out. More realistic options are the one-off charters and leasing arrangements with Gulfstream, and part-share ownership of a plane. I recommend that, now the Concorde is grounded and aged, it's time to get on with what is now the only way to fly. This site, set in a beautifully understated black and gold design, should drive you mad with envy – Arnold Schwarzenegger's got one! John Travolta's got one! Where's mine? – and entertain you at the same time. On one page you can kit out the plane's interior with your own choice of seating, but remember: the real thing is going to be, like, tailor made. On another, you can even check out the aircraft's stats. Features that distinguish the Gulfstream V from the competition are the flying speed (Mach 0.88), the range (Tokyo to LA, anyone?) and the cruising altitude of 50,000ft, which is high above the altitude band used by commercial jets, baby. Put it this way, you ain't going to be circling in this airborne sex machine, you're just going to get there; discreetly, quietly and in style. This cock-shaped jet is a gay boy's dream if ever there was one. EasyJet to Magaluff this is not.

overall rating:	★★★★★
classification:	private jets
updated:	monthly
navigation:	★★★★★
content:	★★★★★
readability:	★★★★★
speed:	★★★★★
US	

SPECIAL FEATURES

News Gulfstream V Breaks High Speed Record on New York to LA flight! You bet it does. On July 24th, the jet broke the record held by rival jet Citation X. The flight, carrying eight passengers and three crew, left New York and finished in LAX four hours and 34 minutes later, breaking the record by almost 15 minutes. Gulfstream has a service centre in Cambridge, so there's no excuse for not having one really, is there? They even have a second-hand page (pre-owned, they call it), and a set of aircraft to choose from. They had a jet there for only $23,000, but it must have been a misprint – mustn't it? Bid and see.

Events Want to have a look at one? Quaff a gin and tonic in one? Have a shag in one? They were there at the Farnborough Air Show, which ran from July 24th to 30th 2000, and they're just about everywhere. They would be; they've got a range of 6,500 nautical miles, don't you know.

Financial Information You think you're loaded because you bought a bottle of Dom Pérignon in February, don't you? Well, this section should give you some food for thought. A Gulfstream jet costs $30 million, and that's before you've even been anywhere.

Charters Shortly on this site you will be able to check real time aircraft availability. Gulfstream have a commitment to get an aircraft to you anywhere in the world within 24 hours. They can even bring one to Croydon. Since the jet can take off with just 4,000ft of runway, you could probably take off from any number of small airports in the UK. If you want to get a feel for what a Gulfstream charter could feel like, rent Pretty Woman.

Gulfstream Store You need cups, mugs, luggage, models, hats, jackets and, of course, golf clubs, all emblazoned with the Gulfstream logo.

Virtual Tour Click on the gold circles on the aircraft plan drawing and you get a 360 degree tour of the aircraft interior, courtesy of an amazing IPIX photograph.

Brochure Drain your office printer of colour by downloading this gigantic, image-packed brochure from Gulfstream. This is the one they'd mail you if you phoned up – unless you had a Scouse accent, that is, in which case they'd hang up. It's enough to make you despise British Airways, conventional airports, boarding passes, baggage carousels and all the crap that comes with normal flights. Save up your $30 million and you'll be there.

The place to drool – in private.

gay

overall rating: ★ ★ ★ ★ ★	
classification: escort service	
updated: frequent	
navigation: ★ ★ ★ ★ ★	
content: ★ ★ ★ ★ ★	
readability: ★ ★ ★	
speed: ★ ★ ★ ★ ★	

www.london-lads.co.uk
London Lads Escorts

I still feel a tiny frisson when I encounter a site which says it contains exceptionally dangerous, shocking or pornographic material. I have never, for fear of being offended, departed from a site yet; indeed, I am more often offended by the rubbish that some people describe as pornography these days. How these entry pages are intended to work remains a mystery. A five-year-old child can click a mouse icon on a 'Yes' box. Some people take the view that five-year-olds are rarely left alone with computers. More often than not these strange people live in the Home Counties, and express surprise when told that 15 per cent of motorists are happy to drive in the absence of insurance, MOT certificates that cover the driving day in question, and correctly fastened seat belts. On council estates, we do things differently.

And London Lads does strike the browser as a council-estate-kind-of enterprise: it's gritty and it's real. These blokes are available for a shag, and there it is. No gloss or glamour surrounds this fact, and if you don't like it, why don't you try www.bbc.co.uk/theteletubbies? The escorts will scarcely be unfamiliar to readers of QX, but there are many others. Most have worked hard at their images and leave it there; others lead you on to inevitable Mancheck payments. The design is neat, sections are marked by icons which show their names with a sweep of the mouse's arrow, and there is information, application forms and all manner of other things that you could want. The site covers greater London.

SPECIAL FEATURES

What's New Who's new on the site, and their pictures, as well as changes to the site structure, entreaties to search, review escorts and an opportunity to give feedback.

Advice to Clients Standard rules apply: see an escort when you're horny, not when you're lonely, and don't pay him out of the money you need for the rent. Wear your glasses. The advice on this site is good, clear and quite extensive. If you have been brought up Catholic, like me, this will bring out your strange mix of uneasiness and respect. My word, these escorts do go through it, don't they?

Advice to Escorts There's a great bit in the Escorts FAQs where they say: 'Is it confidential?' The answer is: 'No of course not, anything that goes on to the world wide web is viewable to all.'

High quality site with no messing about; does exactly what it should.

overall rating:	★ ★ ★ ★ ★
classification:	cosmetic surgery
updated:	monthly
navigation:	★ ★ ★ ★ ★
content:	★ ★ ★ ★ ★
readability:	★ ★ ★ ★ ★
speed:	★ ★ ★ ★ ★
UK	

www.regencyclinic.co.uk
The Regency Clinic

It had to happen – a website where you can make an appointment for a cosmetic surgery consultation, or even run up a fantasy bill totalling the cost of the procedures which most appeal to you. As The Regency Clinic observes: 'Cosmetic Surgery has now entered the mainstream of society. As we start a new millennium our attitudes towards health and beauty are radically different from those of our parents and grandparents.' Quite. Our grandparents didn't butcher themselves out of vanity and greed for youth! There is information on this tasteful, well-structured site about where to find the clinics and how to book a free consultation. You can book a ring-back call online and someone will call you back within an hour. The site offers full information on the procedures, how they work, what they cost, how long it takes for the effect to take, and what the possible complications are: it's absolutely fascinating. They will soon be adding a Before and After section, featuring an online consultation service.

SPECIAL FEATURES

Procedures There aren't many bits of you that The Regency Clinic won't touch. This fascinating page shows an image of a naked man and woman (in sleek, post-cosmetic form), and between them is a list of available procedures. You can choose from standard face lifts, liposuction and breast augmentation techniques, or go for newer operations like fat implants (fill those hollow cheeks), pec and calf implants, penile augmentation and arm lifts. The face-lift subsection is more detailed still, with full information on the reshaping of your nose, brow, chin, lips and ears, and laser resurfacing of your skin. Haven't you heard of a loofah, sweetie? The details on each procedure are breathtakingly full, and the clinic does not pull any punches when it comes to bruising, swelling, metal stitches that hold your scalp in its new position and, er, straightforward physical agony. Find out how many nights in the clinic your procedure requires, whether you need a general, how long you will take to recover and how much it will all cost – or just enjoy the yeuch factor and thank your lucky stars that you don't need any of it.

Instant Quote Whoever thought of this deserves a free lip implant. Choose your procedure, update the page, and you've got your own cosmetic surgery shopping cart! It's just like amazon.co.uk, although the prices are slightly higher.

A fascinating insight into plastic surgery online shopping.

overall rating: ★★★★	
classification: shopping	
updated: continuous	
navigation: ★★★★★	
content: ★★★★★	
readability: ★★★★★	
speed: ★★★	
UK 🔒	

www.bali-rainbow.com
Bali Travel co.

You may not have considered Bali as a gay tourist destination but, increasingly, it is one. There is a good selection of gay bars, beautiful weather and it's dead cheap. This site offers a lot: recommendations, organising transfers to and from the airport, providing cars and island guides, plus providing a rep for the duration of your stay. It offers excellent interactive maps, photography, and descriptions of Bali which capture the island's amazing atmosphere and stunning beauty. Bali Rainbow also have packages to sell you with prices in US$, and you can book online. Rent a private villa with staff and a pool for around $1000 for 14 days.

SPECIAL FEATURES

Bali Recommended Images and descriptions of the island's best hotels, guest houses and villas.

Packages Choose from three prepared packages which include accommodation and flights and numerous services, or go a la carte and design your own trip. Bali Rainbow can handle bookings for any hotel on the island and works with all the airlines which fly to Indonesia.

Beautiful Bali A glimpse, in photographs, of why the place is so special.

If you're going to Bali for a holiday, check this page out first.

www.dirtybastards.com
Dirty Bastards Shop

overall rating: ★★★★
classification: shopping and sex
updated: weekly
navigation: ★★★★★
content: ★★★★★
readability: ★★★
speed: ★★★★★
UK 🔒

This brilliantly designed, rubber-gear website opens with the sounds of phones dialling and a connection being made to the internet. Don't go charging into 'My Computer' to figure out what the hell's going on: you're being wound up. Nice one, boys. There's a great menu, too, from which you can attempt to choose where you want to go but can't because it won't keep still. Dirty Bastards is a company which supplies rubber gear and other stuff (lube, condoms, cockrings, and so on), and it also has an international sex-contacts page. You get insulted in various unoriginal ways as you surf, but even that's entertaining. Affectionately retouched images of men in various states of asphyxiation are somewhat belied by the keen attention to detail shown in the page design.

SPECIAL FEATURES

Workshop The workshop is located near The Globe theatre in London's Bankside (the city's 17th-century red light district), and you can see it online in a panoramic, Shockwave picture. It looks like it's been hit by a missile, but that's the style of these things. You can go there at the listed opening times or by appointment only, finding it first on the Adobe map. You can also make a sleazy appointment and play with the toys on site.

Mailshot Sign up for free goods and services, and make yourself feel like a dirty-rubber bastard when you're checking your email.

Bastards The Bastards Interface is a crosswire which illuminates various images as you sweep the mouse across it. Click on the images to see more; typically, it's an enlarged version of the photo and more information. One section takes you to a set of opening times and locations for the bars Fist, The Backstreet, The Hoist, Sub South, and all the places you already know and love. Other sections take you into the rubber equivalent of Photo-love stories. This section is well-designed, imaginative and horny, and it totally makes the page. Go and have a play.

Dirty Mail An international mail space for you to advertise your desires or respond to those of others.

Web Shop You can order from the Chooser, where you'll find products listed, but it's more fun to look at the action stories and click on the garments shown in them. Happy shopping!

The best of the rubber shopping sites.

www.haleclinic.com
The Hale Clinic

If you want to see a truly sleek and beautiful website, click on this one. The Hale Clinic is situated on Park Crescent, near Regent's Park, and was opened by Theresa Hale in 1987 to combine and integrate the principles of conventional and complementary medicine. The outstanding Nutri Centre in the basement of the complex should stock any product you might wish to buy, including everything that has been recommended for HIV+ individuals. There isn't a shopping-cart facility for this, but Hale probably doesn't need one because their ordering hotline is very efficient, with goods dispatched on the same day. The Nutri Centre also features a huge range of books about

overall rating:	★★★★
classification:	shopping
updated:	continuous
navigation:	★★★★★
content:	★★★★★
readability:	★★★
speed:	★★★★★
UK	

The Hale Clinic, 7 Park Crescent, London W1N 3HE
Tel:020 7631 0156   Fax: 020 7637 3377

health, so again, anything you have heard of and want to buy should be available from them. The Clinic offers a wide range of treatments and, although prices are aimed at the top end of the market, you can be sure that you will be dealt with by specialists of the highest ability. This site has a map which shows the location of the clinic, email services so you can contact the Hale, and a full list of all available therapies. It also features a list of ailments which can be treated at the Hale, so you don't need to go on suffering. There are treatments here for asthma and insomnia, among others, and free advice online.

The real life clinic is glamorous, expensive and beautiful, and this site makes a great virtual match.

www.kwikmed.com
viagra/propecia

This slightly cheaper US site was, at the time of writing, doing the best deals. Fill out the online prescription form (remembering to say that you are suffering from Erectile Dysfunction), and use a credit card to place the order. There is a question and answer page to clear up confusion as to what Viagra actually does, what the possible side effects are and who manufactures it. Pfizer hold an exclusive licence on the manufacture of the drug at present, and you can be sure, using these online ordering facilities, that you are getting the real thing. The drawback of a site such as this is that to take advantage of the lowest prices you have to spend a lot of money on Viagra: $400 for 30 x 100mg pills. The alternative is lying to a doctor, which you've probably done before.

Truth or dare? It's up to you.

overall rating:
★ ★ ★ ★

classification:
online drug sales

updated:
continuous

navigation:
★ ★ ★ ★ ★

content:
★ ★ ★ ★ ★

readability:
★ ★ ★ ★ ★

speed:
★ ★ ★ ★ ★

US

overall rating: ★ ★ ★ ★	
classification: online drug sales	
updated: monthly	
navigation: ★ ★ ★ ★ ★	
content: ★ ★ ★ ★ ★	
readability: ★ ★	
speed: ★ ★ ★ ★ ★	
UK	

www.ukyes.com
M.E.D Clinic

If you can't talk your GP into writing you a prescription for Viagra (and be on the social so it's free, like real erections), you can get it online. On most sites you can also buy the hair-restoring drugs Propecia and Regaine, the weight-control drug Xenical, arthritis relief drug Celebrex and the smoking cessation drug Zyban. Everything is delivered in unalarming packaging, and your credit card bill will be imprinted with a nondescript TLA that everyone at the Credit Card Centre in South End knows screams 'person purchasing porn!!' Sites break down into two main categories: those that charge flat fees for the pills, and those that charge a one-off prescription charge plus delivery, combined with a low per-pill price. The bigger your order, the more you 'save'. It's worth doing your sums to figure the true price of those 100mg pills (of which you only take half, remember), because the one-off prescription fee and delivery charge often come to less in total than the 'inclusive' sites. Compare this to the US site KWIKMED.COM, which offers 10x100mg Viagra at $129.50; which, together with a $65 consultation fee and a $46 international delivery charge, comes to US $240.50 or $12 per 50mg dose. At the current exchange rate that's about £7 a dose, undercutting the UK YES site by 30 per cent. The latest information can be found on the newsgroups at alt.drugs.viagra.

Dig out your school calculator and check this site out, if you want to sniff out the Viagra bargains.

www.regulation-ltd.co.uk
Regulation

It's funny how two specialists like Expectations and Regulation can come up with such different websites. The Regulation site is neat and, built with images from the current catalogue, shows just five categories from which to select. Choose from Rubber, Leather, Bondage, Military and Toys.

SPECIAL FEATURES

Rubber Hooded bodysuit? Shoulder length gauntlets? Tank suit? It's all here, complete with price lists, ordering information, and some fascinating photography that must have taken hours to set up.

Leather Again, images from the catalogue are reproduced here, and they actually look better than their print counterparts. Regulation's extensive leather collection includes leather jeans and chaps, harnesses, underwear, caps and masks. They have a made-to-measure service and they do everything off the peg as well, in regular sizes.

Toys Dr Kaplan is on hand to enlarge your penis – even though, of course, you don't need it.

Ordering Currently by fax, email and phone, though a cart-based service is due.

Even if you don't buy you'll enjoy the images, but Regulation is always worth a trip in real life.

overall rating:
★ ★ ★ ★

classification:
leather & rubber clothing

updated:
monthly

navigation:
★ ★ ★ ★ ★

content:
★ ★ ★ ★ ★

readability:
★ ★ ★

speed:
★ ★ ★ ★ ★

UK

overall rating: ★ ★ ★	
classification: leather & rubber clothing	
updated: monthly	
navigation: ★ ★ ★ ★ ★	
content: ★ ★ ★ ★ ★	
readability: ★ ★ ★	
speed: ★ ★ ★ ★ ★	
UK	

www.expectations.co.uk
Expectations

Lots of little suggestive pics surround the entrance to this gay leather and rubber online sales floor, and you can bet this is one line that Harrods don't stock. You will already have seen the intriguing model they use in their ads, shot in a horny industrial location, and you're probably familiar with the logo they use – an X inside a circle. This page, which elaborates on what Expectations has to offer, is perfect for a sneaky look as you work up the courage to actually go there and try on some masks, harnesses and leather shorts. The clothing is mainly made on the premises in Great Eastern Street, and the company will repair or alter things for you. There's a link to the Hoist, where many of the clothes will be worn – and, during the course of the evening, removed – and standard guest book and site map pages which work well. Expectations speak mysteriously of parties they hold in conjunction with London clubs, but reveal no more, and you can even hire the Expectations shop for your own private use.

SPECIAL FEATURES

Leather Expectations' Premium Range is made from horse hide, no less, and it isn't cheap. Most of what you can imagine buying is here, but there are a few surprises. You can order online, for once in your life supplying truthful measurements and omitting your genital 'aura' so the stuff will actually fit. The ordering is secure and well thought out, considering all the things you need to tell them in order to get everything right, especially in the made-to-measure section. Ring your mum to refresh your memory about what an inside leg is and how to establish a cap size. You can order a catalogue costing £8, but this outlay is deductible from your first order of over £50. Caps, briefs, chaps, harnesses, jackets, masks and hoods are all here, but the photography is not always up to standard. Irritatingly, when you click the thumbnails the new image is often hardly bigger. Who would be tempted into spending £200 on something they couldn't see properly? The standard catalogue shopping dilemma – whether people will buy made-to-measure without seeing the items for themselves – is no better resolved by Expectations than by anyone else. Besides, it's fun to be in the store itself, breathing the concentrated aroma of new leather as you decide. Incidentally, some of the models shown here have the look of newly released Maze prisoners; make up your own mind whether this is a good thing or not. The shorts are great, though; perfect for your sister's wedding.

Rubber Rubber sheets, as we all know, can be robbed from a hospital. But then they're the wrong colour, so you could do worse than invest in the huge black mats that Expectations do. The rubber suits were the most poorly photographed items on the site, which is a shame, because it's clear that Tony and Jonathan, who own and manage the shop, believe in what they're doing. You could always join in their Hosted Chat Session and tell them what you think (last one held on 8th August). Participation brings a 10 per cent discount.

Other You'll find toys, medical surprises (take your blood pressure on Viagra and poppers, anyone? It's the latest thing at sex parties), Tom of Finland gear and such like here.

Personals It remains one of the enduring mysteries of life that all owners of expensive sports cars are pig ugly – and so we find something similar on the gay scene. It appears that if a person has taken the trouble to spend a lot of money kitting out a playroom with everything a boy could want he will, at the same time, be the very last person you'd want to have in it with you. Don't let me stop you.

Models Think you've got what it takes to bring the Expectations gear to life? Send them a pic.

Good taster site which certainly delivers the goods but could perhaps use a dash of Shockwave.

www.shoppingsweetie.com
Shopping Sweetie

The intro to this site is really sweet: 'In the mood for shopping, sweetie? Then you're virtually in the right place. From aromas to pet accessories, vino to videos, you'll find it all here under one virtual roof. Buy from all your favourite names with just one basket, and one checkout and we will pack all of your purchases into just one delivery – direct to your door. No more achy biceps, boys and girls. Just pure simple shopping, sweetie!'

The site is still being developed but it's already offering a pile of stuff to browsers. The site directory shows a mall, complete with loos (soon to be chat rooms) and a vacant lot (want to open up online?) You can buy gift vouchers, and there's a special on at the moment that offers a £10 voucher on spendings of £50 or more. The stores work the same way: you enter one, the products are listed, and you can click on 'charge me sweetie' or 'more info' to get the details on the stuff. Let's go shopping!

SPECIAL FEATURES

The Video Store, The Play Pen and The Book Store Gay movies by Bruce La Bruce, Tanya Wexler, Richard Natale et al, and in the Play Pen poppers come in three-packs for £9. The bookstore has a top 10 and a selection of rooms to choose from, like erotic fiction, fiction and poetry and photography.

overall rating:	★★
classification:	online shopping mall
updated:	continuous
navigation:	★★★★★
content:	★★★★★
readability:	★★
speed:	★★★★★
UK	

www.shoppingsweetie.com

Email us for further information

Obsessions Obsessions is the health and beauty section, where you can buy a Bodi-Tek toning machine, aromatherapy oils for your burner, skin and hair care products, and vitamins. Pricing is pretty much standard retail, but there are extra products that you might not have known about, like a Bodi-Tek face rejuvenator.

Music Store, Cards, Toys offers a selection of titles, but it's somewhat limited. It's not the best place to get music online, unless exactly what you want pops up in the window. The card section suffers from the same limitation; one of the fun aspects of buying cards is browsing, and here you can't even see the cards. However, the Toy store, offering black leather collars in which to imprison your friends, parents or colleagues, works better and is more fun.

Tickets You can buy tickets to Wild Fruit and Kinky Booty here.

The Gallery Art gallery offering painters' wares online. To be expanded.

A good idea which, when fully developed, will be a cool place to shop.

OTHER SITES OF INTEREST

Gay Zoo
www.gayzoo.com
Powerful, gay-led search engine with links to everything from entertainment to employment and personal homepages. These personal pages can be really amazing, and a complete time sink if you get into them. This is a highly organized, Yahoo-style site which should take you where you want to go.

Prowler
www.prowler.co.uk
A shopping site from Millivres Prowler group, now under construction.

Man Around
www.manaround.com
A cool holiday site dealing with Europe, South Africa, Thailand, Ibiza, Sydney Mardi Gras, and all the typical destinations (Sitges, Mykonos, Gran Canaria and Barcelona). Last-minute-deal prices looked good, with flights from all major UK airports at decent times and free extra-night offers.

Outlet
www.outlet.co.uk
You may remember the real-life Outlet which operated from various premises, such as over Clone Zone in Old Compton Street and then from an office by The Box. Now it's online, offering a residential accommodation matching service and a holiday accommodation service.

freaks, liars and christians

In theory, the net is a medium which you can use to launch yourself upon the world. Production costs are tiny compared to the processes an organisation will have to endure in order to bring you a newspaper, book, film, record or television show. Unlike all these mediums, a website does not have to be a collaboration, either. It can be the work of just one person. It is still a new medium, and while you can't, for example, pump images to the world of yourself having sex without legal consequences, it is open to everyone and there are few other restrictions. The challenge that faces amateur web-contestants, however, is how to make the site interesting for other people. The net is exciting because anything could happen. It is conceivable that there could be a famous website which was so cleverly done that people felt they had to tune in every week, as if to a TV show. Nothing of this sort exists at the moment, and the ceaseless array of personal pages, most of which haven't had much money or time spent on them, are mostly a bore. Here are some of those which aren't boring, and which, for one reason or another, prove entertaining. We've tried to think about all the different purposes people are trying to accomplish with their personal sites, and bring you something from each category.

www.pstafford.com
Paul Stafford's site

This is an exemplary site. In his descriptions, Paul seems to have realised that people from all over the world can see his site, so he explains everything effectively. With a simple, unpretentious style throughout, this site is the antithesis of the mystery projected by Zerocrop, and worlds away from the fuck-me-but-fuck-you pages on barebackcentral. What is excellent about Paul's page is the way he puts technology to work and acknowledges that you might not be that interested in him and his life. Many of the sites I looked at featured people who were saying, 'Weh-hey, we're on Web Cam, look at us!' You wonder why they bothered, and of course, there is no more reason to look at people you don't know through a Web Cam lens than there is to watch them from a table in a café. As I reviewed all these sites, I began to realise how boring it must be to be a stalker. Then I clicked here and it wasn't so terrible. Instead of taking the look-at-me route, Paul sets himself up as a place to begin with this interesting new technology and recommends some great alternative Web Cam pages. As the refresh rate improves over the coming years and your processor improves with each new generation of computer, it could be as good as TV. The mind boggles with the possibilities. A Web Cam in Joan Collins' downstairs loo? In the Queen's TV snug? The first celebrity to put their life online will certainly intrigue the nation, and it would be possible to launch a TV show called something like Salon and show a bunch of amazing people having dinner or whatever, and we could all tune in to watch.

overall rating:	★ ★ ★ ★ ★
classification:	personal web cam site
updated:	continuous
navigation:	★ ★ ★ ★ ★
content:	★ ★ ★ ★ ★
readability:	★
speed:	★ ★ ★ ★ ★
UK	

However, for the rest of us, the central problem with such sites remains unsolved: how the hell do you make it interesting? Even the life of a celebrity is, no matter how Hello! might paint it, full of mundane things, none of them worth a sentence of virtual conversation. Paul Stafford tells us he's been painting his house, but it's difficult to be interested in someone painting their house even when it's your best mate. Even when it's you. And it's not just the lives that aren't gripping; it's the style of sites, the photography, and so on. The difference between a set of professional photographs and a pack of 36 knocked off at Snappy Snaps is horrifying. As pleasant as your feelings towards Paul Stafford might be, it's soon time to go.

As he points out, there is a Web Cam ring which is worth exploring. After a time, though, you start to get the picture: you are watching strangers live, and if they are doing any nudity or sex they will have to charge you for it. 'Well,' you might retort, 'that's all Big Brother was, and that pulled five-million viewers.' But would you have watched Big Brother had it lacked the cruelty of nomination, the moment of eviction and the prize money? Of course you wouldn't. Unless you're a stalker. So, unless you are blatantly authoring a web page in order to arrange sex, the only way to make it interesting is to be extraordinarily gorgeous, famous, powerful or psychotic.

Search the web cam ring at www.gaywebcams.org for more excruciatingly normal men.

A great site if you are thinking through how best to present yourself to a cruel world.

www.zerocrop.com
Zerocrop

overall rating:	★ ★ ★ ★ ★
classification:	bondage
updated:	no updating
navigation:	★ ★ ★ ★ ★
content:	★ ★ ★ ★ ★
readability:	n/a
speed:	★ ★ ★ ★ ★
UK 🔒	

This is perfection, and exactly how a personal sex site should look. You never actually get to see Zerocrop's face, body or cock. Instead, the images, music and design conjure up the kind of fantasy man you want: muscular, sexy, powerful, remote. The site oozes sex and mystery, and Zerocrop takes advantage of the internet's location outside of time and space. Where is he? What does he do? How did he make this site? What's he like in bed? Since these questions have no answers, he grows incrementally hornier. The music is great and you can buy it by sending Zerocrop £10 for his Ain't No Wanker CD, though it is beyond doubt that the whole point of this site is to point out to you, once and for all, that you are a wanker. As gay men all know but rarely admit, achieving the kind of sex you really want and persuading the kind of men you really want to do it to you takes some doing. It's an area of life that no-one will help you with, least of all other gay men, and that's one of the reasons why backrooms, cruising areas and internet rooms are full, and the reason why a site like Zerocrop's can seem so exciting.

The site is excellent because it captures with precision the kind of gay man who is a great fuck but also despicably cruel. Zerocrop is a fantasy, a Class 1 pisstaker. If you don't want to have sex with him he thinks you're a wanker, and if you do want to have sex with him then he thinks you're a wanker. No-one can win except Zerocrop, and the fact that Carl Jung and Sigmund Freud figured out how people get this way is of no help to you

and your hard-on tonight. If you wish to leave a message for him do so, but of course he won't be in touch (and judging by the message centre, some of you are dead naïve). If you actually do meet him, it will be bondage – and don't expect a lesson.

Watch the shockwave images, listen to the music, buy the CD, get horny and start a site of your own!

http://www.the-pns-brothers.com/markzsitez/content.html
Skinhead Mark

Ever thought of launching yourself as a porn star? That's what Skinhead Mark has done, and it works. He announces himself as 27 years old and living in North London with a good, fit, tattooed body and a nice, fat, uncut, tattooed cock. He is not camp, has no attitude, and is 100 per cent active. Then he allows you to download a free movie of him wanking in his Union Jack T-Shirt. It's all very enjoyable and well put-together, and it's a perfect tease, because once you have seen the free video you naturally want to see more. That's when you whip out your credit card and pay for access to his private porn collection, which features – you guessed it – him.

SPECIAL FEATURES

The Movies New movies are added every seven days. Each one is shot on a camcorder in a variety of places in Mark's home and elsewhere. You can take a three-day trial for about a fiver, or sign up for 30 days at US$14.95. Then you can enter the download pages and choose from 90 videos which play on QuickTime. Click on a still from the movie to begin the download. The quality is excellent and all the movies were horny. Each takes about 20 minutes to download at 56k. The only problem I had with this page is that it crashes, and you have to be patient because you can't download more than one film at a time.

overall rating:	★★★★
classification:	personal porn site
updated:	weekly
navigation:	★★★★★
content:	★★
readability:	n/a
speed:	★★★★★
UK 🔒	

Mark's Music An intriguing addition to the pages – Mark's own choice of tracks. You can listen to his favourite tunes by following the link to music stream, which plays back in WinAmp.

Mark's Links A list of the dirtiest sites Mark has found to date, and a bit of music.

Excellent personal porn broadcasting page.

www.wannasleepover.com
Want to Sleep Over?

This is a great example of a really slutty site with no pretension, censoring or narcissism. It's similar to Paul's site in a sense, except that this one's about sex. What we have here is an average guy who is playing the voyeur and exhibitionist game. He doesn't have a great body and, in a way, the whole site reeks of sadness and loneliness. Still, the calm, colourful and even presentation works. I don't know why images of ordinary domestic interiors should convey such sadness and seem so remote, but they do. A melancholy hangs over this site and others like it, as you gaze in puzzlement at these men who, while not being really attractive or in good shape, want to exhibit themselves to strangers for nothing and advertise their home-made flicks at what can only be described as humorous prices. Offering for sale a tape of yourself wanking is at once funny and cool and tragic, or just plain tragic if you need the money. It's a waste of time, but in another sense you are there looking at them, so they have received something.

overall rating:	
classification:	web cam page
updated:	daily
navigation:	★ ★ ★ ★ ★
content:	★ ★ ★ ★ ★
readability:	★ ★ ★ ★
speed:	
US	

SPECIAL FEATURES

Some Fun He gets onto the bed, strips off, and has a wank.

Walk in the Park When you think about it, this is clever. It's simply a series of shots of Mr Come Over hanging out by a tree and cruising you, the viewer. He's acting out that aspect of the gay man who wants to do this, so he's really just a mirror.

The glint in his eye throughout the site suggests a somewhat greater level of thought and awareness than perhaps you'd initially expect.

Underwear Do you want to purchase some cum-stained undies? Not only can you do that here with your credit card; you can also select from two-day old, three-day old and four-day old underwear, in different styles. It's like Harrods, really.

Curiously matter-of-fact web cam page. I blame Bill Gates.

www.barebackcentral.net/members
Bareback Webring Members

I am not going to go on about the surrealness of ordinary citizens presenting their faces, bodies, cocks and interests to the world via the internet. It is strange, it is surreal, and nobody knows what the psychological consequences are. Possibly I am making it all sound needlessly sinister, but I think that the average person does see a sinister side to the internet and wonders where it is all going.

There are plenty of examples here of men who have chosen to put themselves online, and they all look harmless enough. They stand in contrast to the elusive Zerocrop, and as examples of the simplest way to approach online sex – show your face and body, say what you want and leave it at that. It's unpretentious, inexpensive and straightforward. You don't feel like you're going to have to play a game with these people; it's either yes or no. Zerocrop is exciting but empty, while you can deal with these people in a single email. There's no two ways about it; using the internet for sex is hard work. It's harder than a club and probably the biggest time-sink since cruising.

As simple as net-sex gets.

overall rating: ★★★	
classification: bareback webring	
updated: no updating	
navigation: ★★★★	
content: ★★★	
readability: ★★★	
speed: ★★★★	
UK	

gay

overall rating: ★	
classification: web cam page	
updated: daily	
navigation: ★ ★ ★ ★ ★	
content: ★ ★ ★ ★ ★	
readability: ★	
speed: ★ ★ ★ ★ ★	
US 🔒	

http://voyeur.badpuppy.com/jonthon
Jonathan and Jasons's Web Cam page

For the sake of thoroughness I have included a page showing self-love and narcissism run riot. It's not a bad page as far as design and tech goes, but there is something odd about a page where two guys have chosen to buy digital cameras, film themselves wanking and then offer the resulting videotapes for sale to anyone on a website for $25 a pop. Hello? They are far from being the only people who are doing this, and it is the downside of a new technology. In the absence of intelligence, realism, objectivity or common sense, people are making fools of themselves online. It's not even funny after the first time. This site has none of the sense of Paul Stafford's site, none of the deadly sexual charm of Zerocrop, and none of the honesty of the bareback pages. It will make you laugh. But not for long.

Mindlessly self-indulgent. Who are these people?

www.nakedtony.com
Naked Tony's page

Ever noticed how America is full of guys named Kirk, Brent, Todd and Scott? There is a reason for it, and it's this: a lot of men's mothers are closet gay men and the naming of their sons is the only way they can express their sexuality. In this review I endeavour to cover every conceivable application of the Web Cam and personal page technology, and this is an example of International Unsolicited Online Stripping. Only 1,200 categories to go; are you still with me?

This is Tony's fantasy page, really. What is so breathtaking about it is that out of him and all his friends and everyone he has met and photographed and put here online, there isn't one image worth looking at. It just shows how much effort goes into professional magazine shots. However, the bravado of it all amazed me, and I loved Tony's Exhibitionist Page, in which he and his mates take their clothes off in public in the style of Madonna's book Sex. I bought an Adult Check for the purpose of this review; you need one to tour this section and for some reason it was worth it (novelty value, really), in a way it isn't on all those professional sex pages.

One man and his mates in cahoots. Almost admirable in its complete and utter pointlessness.

overall rating:	★
classification:	web cam page
updated:	daily
navigation:	★ ★ ★ ★ ★
content:	★ ★ ★ ★ ★
readability:	★
speed:	★ ★ ★ ★ ★
US	

OTHER SITES OF INTEREST

Gay Web Rings

A web ring is a collection of sites which are all related. Typically, there is a web master who oversees who is in and who is out. When a site is a member of a web ring, there will usually be a box at the bottom of the page telling you so, and showing you buttons for the next and previous five or links to the web master. The best way to learn about web rings, which are there to help organise the net for you, is to go to one and see what it's like. At www.hemen.de (de denotes a German website), you'll find the homepage for the Gay Skinhead Ring, but he is also a member of the Gay S&M Ring. On the homepage of the Gay Skinhead Ring it tells you what it is, how it works, how to join, how to use it and what to expect. There are web rings for just about everything you could think of. The bareback web ring, for example, is at www.barebackcentral.net.

celebrity Morgue
www.celebritymorgue.com

Delightful images of dead celebrities, including Elvis, Marilyn Monroe, Kurt Cobain and Pol Pot. Entertainment for, possibly, a horrible drug comedown.

magazines and books

What do gay people read? Well, exactly the same stuff as anyone else, really. But there are now enough titles aimed at gay men and lesbians for us to speak of a market. Some of the titles are free and, reading these, you can only conclude that there's even less to being gay than the frequently advertised features of sex, drugs, music and the gym. The magazines offered for sale are usually better. Gay Times is the long-suffering title of the gay publishing world. Meanwhile, the Pink Paper has recently become a newsstand title. Attitude devotes itself to fashion, music, men and gay lifestyle while in the free market, Boyz is brilliantly incomprehensible and, judging by its décor, buzzing on a kind of drug that you just can't get anymore. QX is just plain daft, but endearingly so. Diva, newer than the Gay Times, is better, and for a lesbian readership, while Axiom caters for those who are HIV positive or wish to know about the latest advances in HIV medicine and general health. However, if you already buy these magazines off the shelves or liberate them from the dark corners of London gay bars, you won't really find new material for them online. Then again, if you don't buy them, why would you look for an online version? At some level, the designers of the sites are aware of this problem and the only magazine which has faced it squarely, in our view, is DNA. The magazine complements the website and vice versa.

Moving away from 'gay' titles, the internet opens up not only places to buy books but also vast libraries containing all the classics free, and, of course, the growing new world of online-only magazines, fanzines and netzines.

www.blairmag.com
Blairmag

Blair mag is that rare thing: a totally funny gay fanzine that's purely about being gay and what it means. I was in fits looking at the title page for Blair 6: hello from Blair; Carol Channing; puppetry; cats; electric wheelchairs. Blair 6 is the 'Broadway birdcage and handicapped inspired issue', and it works like mad. Blissfully funny, rude and fresh, it's like a top TV show you have to tune into every few days. There are wonderful games to play, like 'gay or Euro trash', brilliant new angles on the gay life ('is she a lesbian or just German?', they ask in one of their older games), and intelligent reviews of the entertainment biz. When reviewing Cats they say: 'the idea that every night a few blocks away from us there were people running around dressed as alley cats and singing was too hilarious to pass up.' In a feature on sewing: 'Making a pillow is a relaxing activity you should try. All you need to know how to do is stitch, which is totally easy.' All the back issues are here online and each has at least one diverting and amusing article.

Compulsive gay magazine with – gasp! – a sense of humour.

| overall rating: |
| ★ ★ ★ ★ ★ |

| classification: |
| magazine |

| updated: |
| weekly |

| navigation: |
| ★ ★ ★ ★ ★ |

| content: |
| ★ ★ ★ ★ ★ |

| readability: |
| ★ ★ ★ ★ |

| speed: |
| ★ ★ ★ ★ ★ |

| US |

overall rating: ★ ★ ★ ★ ★	
classification: gay magazines	
updated: monthly	
navigation: ★ ★ ★ ★ ★	
content: ★ ★ ★ ★	
readability: ★ ★ ★ ★	
speed: ★ ★ ★ ★ ★	
UK R	

www.dnamag.com
DNA Magazine

If Queer Company is style incarnate, DNA stands at the opposite end of the gay spectrum – it's strangely insightful and brutally honest. Presented in large type with primary coloured boxes, and coloured in like a children's magazine (or like Viz), DNA is also, as the website itself exclaims, funny: 'there's been nothing funny about being gay until now...' That the gay community should be so humourless is sensationally depressing, when you think about it; DNA, 'filled with hilarious news, gossip, opinion and nonsense', is the answer. It was started three years ago by Laurence and Steve, and 'has grown from small beginnings to something very small and struggling'. Perhaps the biggest joke of all is at the expense of the other magazines, like Diva, Attitude and Gay Times, which strain for coolness and never get anywhere near it, while DNA effortlessly occupies cool central and doesn't harp on about it. Now that is cool.

Indeed, DNA is so laid back that they pretty much expect that you will be sending in your own stories, ideas and opinions, which they will then insert in the mag without so much as a single word subbed. I have found that this process doesn't normally work with Vanity Fair. A phone-dial style box allows you to navigate through the site, but it opens with a list of the main articles on which you can click straight away.

SPECIAL FEATURES

DNA News You can grasp the DNA style from even one article. At the time of review the DNA News Headline was that Prince William was gay: 'Top royal piece of crumpet Prince William has been caught up in a scandal after his grandma embroiled him in a sexual slur. After attending another celebration party for her 100th birthday the Queen Mum was asked by reporters if she'd had a good time. She replied: "Why yes, thank you dearie, I had a super time. I sat next to that adorable William, and as you know he's very gay."' How can anyone argue with that?

DNA Guys DNA guys are 'improved formula with added XXX', and even the registration process offers a dose of humour. I suspect that the user name and passwords given me were the same for everyone. Without a doubt, this is the best free gallery of all the UK sites. Check out the photographs or read a dirty story.

Personals Click this and you are taken to www.one-and-only.com, one of the better online dating services. Choose your country and city, decide what you are looking for and check the ads. It's easy and free to join up, but sadly the DNA humour does not reach these parts. It's a dry experience which will have you snapping at your back button in seconds.

DNA Shop Where did they get that gorgeous blue background? Anyway, they've got those aromas here, and some dildos and pouches and shorts and coffee table books and gay videos and DVDs and Billy dolls and sex aids and toys and vibrators and gay travel guides and all the rest of it. Go and buy Florist Billy now.

Subscribe to DNA Be mad not to. Still available for free in some places, it's far better to have your own copy delivered to your door in embarrassing see-through wrapping. Only £15.95 for 12 months! Amazing.

DNA Links To surprising places that you'd never have visited without the proper expert guidance of the personages behind this extraordinary magazine.

The People Behind DNA Lovely write-ups about the small but savagely energetic staff. The company is run by children under five, as you can clearly see from these online photographs. Nevertheless, they can all read and write to a high standard, and lay out pages in QuarkXpress.

The best fun in online gay magazines.

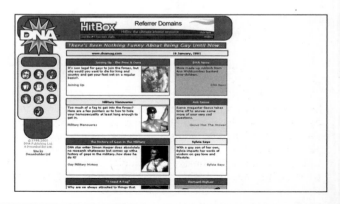

www.queercompany.com
Queer Company

overall rating:	★★★★★
classification:	on-line magazine
updated:	weekly
navigation:	★★★★★
content:	★★★★★
readability:	★★★★★
speed:	★★★★★
UK R	

'Nobody here will be telling you how to think,' says Jonathan Keane, the Content Director of this brand new online magazine. Queer Company is an intriguing, if embryonic, departure from the dated muscle and dance onslaught of print gay magazines. It will be interesting, however, to see who chooses to advertise on the site, since whatever you do in gay land you always seem to end up with some kind of dated muscle and dance onslaught. The site looked glorious without flashing advertisements; it launched, revenue permitting, in October, and we hope it maintains its searing charm once the world knows about it.

The site has a clean, simple style, with carefully selected colours and a minimum of moving parts – which all work. Less is more. You can choose from affairs, society, holiday, culture, scene, style, well-being, finance, and homes. There were a few navigation dead ends on preview showing, but the writing was excellent, the navigation sensible and crisp, and the overall purpose revealed slowly. A site with suspense is a step forward, and it makes you stop and think how fast the internet could become the media trip. Content consists of 200 or 250 snap pieces on Bars, Clubs and Music, but you will find opinion valued over review, and photography designed to denigrate not promote. Cynicism about the homosexual stalemate which triumphed through the 1990s is nicely balanced with constructive clawing at what should come next. Between the lines, the flatness of other gay, online realities is stylishly exposed, and the site works like a well-oiled machine – it needs no propping up with tepid tactics like chat rooms, guest books and visitor clocks. Benchmark browsing.

SPECIAL FEATURES

Scene This section provides excellent coverage of the whole country but focuses on one or two bars and dusts them down, reminding you why you need to go. The archive is currently empty but that's all right. The site has only just launched. The scene guide covers bars, clubs, restaurants, shopping, hotels and you can even post your own review of that cheeky backroom bar, unknown gay friendly country pub or even the phone box where your favourite prostitute places his cards. It's your scene.

Culture With clear-eyed coverage of almost everything, such as film and theatre, concerts, art and books, you can put that Guardian guide in the recycle bin. Buy things here via bol.com.

Style Fashion reviews, with purchasing via www.luxlook.com.

Holiday One exciting destination is presented as you open up the holiday section, but to your left at least a dozen slightly cryptic reviews await your click. Good reviews, good links and writers who, it would seem, have actually been.

Finance The page offers general money advice and has guides on savings, mortgages and sharetrading. Anyone for a pink chequebook?

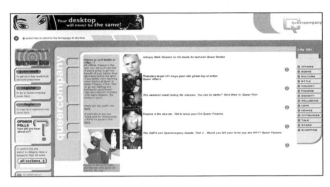

Society A guide to the happening events of this world. At the time of review, it featured a fun description of the MSN party for Madonna's recent London concert.

Well Being This section benefits from the fact that it could address itself to just about anything that promotes (or impedes) well being. Exercise, diet, and general health feature, but features also look at religion and SAD. You can also read the queries (sic) sent to on-line agony aunt Adele, who is certain to secure fame to equal that of Mystic Meg. Told you it wasn't your typical gay site.

Love An embryonic site which asks for your email address.

Homes A fashionable site focusing on the more obscure bits and pieces in the house, like the pouffe, the Jacuzzi and the bunk beds. Where do these people live?

City Guides These bright fresh guides are like martinis – dry as air – and the mesh city guide is sure to be copied onto plenty of private home pages. Click View/Source if you like, but you won't get the HTML code, heh heh. Make your own page, you naughty pilfering thing, you. The guides cover Europe and New York.

Talk Fun, gossipy articles about just about everything, from being a gay parent to love and celebrities. Enter the chat room here.

Stars Your horoscopes. This could be your week to steal a car.

Shopping If you don't know what to buy you need to get someone, quick, to help you. Queer Company's shopping guide can prevent fashion faux pas, and it brings you new products you may not have known existed. You can buy the lot online.

Makes Gay Times look round about as hip as The Daily Mail. Get there.

www.axiomgay.com
Axiom

overall rating: ★ ★ ★ ★	
classification: gay magazines	
updated: continuous	
navigation: ★ ★ ★ ★ ★	
content: ★ ★ ★ ★ ★	
readability: ★ ★ ★ ★	
speed: ★ ★ ★ ★ ★	
UK	

This site pretty much reproduces the contents of the free print magazine aimed at HIV positive men or, indeed, anyone who wants to keep up with developments relating to HIV and AIDS. The page opens with the news in brief, quick links to get your Axiom subscription, and a list of the page's 16 subsections. Check out Axiom's page for job opportunities as well as personal contacts, gay chat and online shopping. The gay chat room feature leads you to the gay.com chat room, which so far is the only one that ever has anyone in it! A 12-month subscription to Axiom costs £28 and you can order one online.

SPECIAL FEATURES

TV Guide This is the only magazine site I found which offered this useful service! It's increasingly common to find that information we were once all happy to pay for is free online, and here you can print out any channel's guide for the coming week and even get alternative ITV regions (what's on in Scotland at 10 tonight, then?) Radio and satellite channels are also listed.

The Browser Reproduces the articles from the current edition of Axiom, so you don't have to sit on the night bus piled high with Boyz, QX and Axiom, wondering whether that man with the machete opposite you has twigged that you're gay. Escape unharmed from this and other uncomfortable urban situations by reading everything you want online.

Travel Link to EasyJet and their confusing one-way fares, and a review of Berlin and Bilbao. Travel reviews change monthly.

Music and Clubbing This is a really excellent resource for club news and little bits of news and gossip. Short, sharp pieces that get you up to date.

HIV News Plenty of information, as you'd expect from Axiom, about HIV, along with reports, articles and information on living with HIV and mixing recreational and anti-HIV drugs. As usual, moving pieces of real-life stories mix with information and news.

A full-on site which is better than the magazine.

www.boyznow.com
Boyz Magazine

Boyz, the free magazine famed for its tasteful coverage of the gay scene and excellence in journalism to rival The Spectator, is now online. This bright, breezy and 100 per cent unapologetic online version of the paper is in most respects preferable to the print version. You can't flick an electronic image on a monitor, and you can't wrap up birthday gifts in the escort ad pages, but you can avoid the sections of Boyz which irritate you, like the invariably hideous 'backroom boy' and the worthless Dear Doc advice. Instead, focus on what Boyz is good at: scene listings, news and the latest fragrance, without which you will surely die.

SPECIAL FEATURES

Scene News Brief news for London, Birmingham, Manchester and Regional. Quickly digestible pieces on what's going on in your local scene.

Scene Listings The complete guide to the UK scene, featuring a Central, West, North, East and South guide to the London scene. Contains addresses, telephone numbers, opening hours and websites.

Web Cams and Home Pages A selection of the nation's web cam self-promoters and those who have created their own home pages for your anonymous enjoyment.

overall rating:
★ ★ ★ ★

classification:
magazine

updated:
weekly

navigation:
★ ★ ★ ★ ★

content:
★ ★ ★ ★ ★

readability:
★ ★ ★

speed:
★ ★ ★ ★ ★

UK   R

Web Chat It's a pity this chat room was deserted, since it looked just as good as the www.gay.com model. Perhaps it will evolve into a little-known but smart web outlet, used by those who wish to leave gay.com to the dotcommoners. There you go, I've sewn the seed.

Message Board Simple and elegant message boards with categories for sex right now or later with Mr Right. Chat rooms are more popular than message boards because you can chat in real time, but your message board note is there 24-hours a day and you don't know who is going to see it.

Meet Market Pick your location within the UK and cruise the personal ads to see if there's anything that takes your fancy. There are hundreds of ads and few ways to distinguish between the people other than using the obvious cues of age, description or the sound of a name. Some people think it's shallow to take an interest in a person's height, cock size and location, but th simple truth is that on all these services every individual is faced with an overwhelming number of choices. You have to decide somehow, don't you?

Backrooms A selection of well-presented, free galleries with good navigation and reasonable speed. It's not as strong a selection as the DNA Gallery, but still worth a peek if you need to flinch into a tissue after an unsuccessful night trying to pull. This section includes hundreds of links to the most surprising and diverse sites, and also private web cam sites, so you can be Big Brother without the assistance of Channel 4. Maybe Southern Comfort will sponsor you anyway.

Also, check out the www.boyztravel.com site for travel guides, bookings and the Planet Gay calendar.

A world you won't find in Boyz print version.

gay

overall rating: ★ ★ ★
classification: gay magazines
updated: continuous
navigation: ★ ★ ★
content: ★ ★ ★
readability: ★ ★
speed: ★ ★ ★ ★
UK

www.gaytimes.co.uk
Gay Times/DIVA

Gay Times is a well-known publication, but in terms of personals, chat rooms and style this site doesn't really score. It's only included out of necessity, really. To give them their due, they say: 'in the new year we will be launching an entirely new website reflecting the full range of products and resources from the MPG Group following the merger of Europe's two leading gay companies.' And there we were thinking Europe's two leading gay companies were British Airways and the Cameron Mackintosh group.

SPECIAL FEATURES

Chat I am looking forward to the new site because The Meet Market, the Gay Times chat room, wasn't working, and the Blue

Room, a chamber for discussion about gay issues, was always empty. Strangely, these symptoms did not affect Diva Chat, which seduced me with message lines like 'ooh maz I really want to pinch your arse!' My mother told me to be a lesbian and she was right all along, sob. There's a lot of discussion here about Claire, who had just arrived in the Big Brother house at the time of review. 'I would nominate her to get away from her voice', says one dyke. It all seems so long ago now.

Let's hope the new site is better!

gay

overall rating: ★ ★ ★	
classification: listings	
updated: haphazard	
navigation: ★ ★ ★ ★	
content: ★ ★ ★ ★	
readability: ★ ★ ★ ★	
speed: ★ ★ ★ ★ ★	
UK	

www.qxmag.co.uk
QX Magazine

So, one day you find you're housebound, or tied up and unable to escape, or just too damn stoned to move and you don't have the latest QX! You hyperventilate: how can you call yourself a homosexual when you have no idea what's going on in this town?! Are you even really gay without a copy of QX? Help! And so on. But fear not, because those charming persons behind London's long-running and fabulously unreadable listings magazine have put the whole thing online. Lovely, pull-down menus show you rapidly where everything is, and there's a nice image of the current cover (almost the current one) to browse. Club and bar news and weekly features are copied verbatim from the mag, and all the regular features are here. Phew. You are gay after all.

SPECIAL FEATURES

What's on this Week Nightly clubs and bars reviewed, with times, locations and prices. You can't go wrong with this most official of London's gay club guides. Choose your night and receive opening times, addresses, dress codes and prices.

Music Features The QX take on the sounds pouring out of clubs and pubs, and what's being played most where, by whom, and when.

QX Picture Gallery A collection of completely innocent nude stills of, you guessed it, blokes. These never seem to change, but at least they're free and you don't get pestered for worthless Mancheck accounts every 25 seconds, or continuously have to squash dodgy teen pop-up boxes.

QX Links Pages Useful links to most of the club pages, like the Trade, Fist and G.A.Y home pages, and their own selection of personal pages which, sometimes, don't exist.

Even more childish, pornographic and insane than the print copy. Delete your cookies before your dad gets in.

OTHER SITES OF INTEREST

Amazon

www.amazon.co.uk

The market leader in online book-selling, music, DVD and games. They have everything, and are the only company which advertises on TV. That should make you think twice about placing orders with them, because we all know how much TV-time costs, don't we? Bear in mind that, if you decide to return something to any online retailer, you can use the postal calculator at www.royalmail.co.uk to find out the postal charge. Just enter the weight and you get the answer.

WHSmith

www.whsmith.co.uk

Watch out for deceptively high Amazon prices. Check out WHSmith before you click 'complete your order'. WHSmith do all the same music, DVD and games, too. It's boring to research

this but the two companies charge differently for postage, so find out about it and save! For example, during a test purchase enquiry on 25 September 2000, I wanted five copies of the party game book All About Me by Phillip Keel. Amazon were offering it at £7.66, so their total with postage of £5.11 came to £43.41. But on WHSmith the book was priced at £6.43, and they were doing free postage and packing on orders over £20, so the order was only £32.15 – a saving of 25 per cent, or £11. Enough for four pints of Guinness, basically. So it is worth checking. Remember, if you are overcharged by Amazon you can return the product within 30 days for a no-quibble refund and re-order from WHSmith.

Guttenberg Books
www.guttenberg.com/
Being gay is not all about sex and shopping. Sometimes you just want to sit at home with a book, and this site has 10,000 free ones to offer. If the book has come out of copyright – like, for example, everything written by Mark Twain or HG Wells – it is sure to be here. Download the ZIP file, open it up and read on screen or on your printout.

health

Though gay men are notorious for smoking, drinking and drugging themselves silly, it's rare for any gay man to be uninterested in health – even if it's only his appearance he's trying to protect. With more disposable income and more free time than their child-rearing counterparts, gay men are the natural consumers of organic food, vitamins, supplements, health magazines and those weird Bodi-Tek machines – or do they just buy Men's Health for the picture of the guy on the cover? I wouldn't dream of trying to decipher the murky motivations, but what's for sure is that there's no better place to learn about what's available in these areas than on the world wide web.

In addition, of course, there are the issues of HIV, AIDS and other sexually transmitted infections. Of course, if you type HIV or AIDS in your Yahoo you'll get the whole web and his wife, so this chapter directs you to the best sites, which feature up-to-the-minute news and articles from leading medical journals. What the internet excels at is bringing you new, thought-provoking material which helps you to frame your questions and directs your attention to matters of which you might have been unaware. Whether the sites are huge and complex, feature controversial figures like Professor Duesburg arguing that HIV never killed anybody, or deliver the latest drug news from Glaxo Wellcome, there is much to be learned from them. The virtual journey into health is one of the most rewarding that you can take online.

overall rating: ★ ★ ★ ★ ★	
classification: medical	
updated: hourly	
navigation: ★ ★ ★ ★ ★	
content: ★ ★ ★ ★ ★	
readability: ★ ★ ★ ★ ★	
speed: ★ ★ ★ ★ ★	

US

www.aegis.com
The Largest HIV/AIDS site in the world: AIDS Education Global Information

This page opens with the HIV Daily Briefing, a collection of up-to-the-minute news articles and briefings. Here you can find information from AIDS conferences, drug trials, press releases and scientific studies. With 750,000 documents in the database, AEGIS is the best place online to get to grips with conventional medical thinking on AIDS and HIV. The current view remains the one expressed in the early 1980s by Professor Gallo: that infection with a sexually transmitted agent, HIV, damages the immune system and that the immune system, thus sabotaged, cannot fight any of the 29 diseases grouped under the term AIDS. In the light of Professor Mbeki's statements about the role of HIV in African AIDS, and the Durban Declaration, scientists on the AEGIS site have put together the most concrete and complete refutation of any idea that HIV might not be the cause of AIDS, and these documents make for provocative and detailed reading. This site is immensely detailed, and the triumph of the designers lies in its effective organisation. As so often happens with the internet, the information, should it be presented in a book, would be so voluminous that you'd probably put it down, rest your arms and watch Neighbours instead. You don't really know the extent of what you're being shown online; you only see one page at a time. This makes it work. Read on, remembering that this information is 'designed to support, not replace, any relationship you have with a doctor'.

SPECIAL FEATURES

Key Topics – The Basics 'Newly infected? Begin here.' Clicking this takes you to a hugely useful page for those panicked about an HIV positive blood test. Don't panic! You're probably not going to die or even get sick for 20 years. This section, written by an HIV positive person, is a great guide to how to tell or not tell people, changing sexual behaviour, beginning to understand treatment options and not destroying your faith and hope. There is plenty here about opportunistic infections, viral load and T cell counts, along with all the other data you will have to come to terms with.

Treatment, Prevention and Exposure Issues Everything you need to know about ATZ, protease inhibitors, new treatments, combination therapy, condoms and lube, exposure risks and so on. The site has suggestions for 'what to do if the condom breaks', and tells you what to expect when you've just been infected. It discusses the blood tests and blood transfusions, and has heaps of information on the 11 HIV drugs that are currently available. I found the section on the drugs extremely helpful, since the site will tell you how they work, what the side effects are and how they can be combined. Indeed, this site goes into enormous detail without ever losing its footing. As long as you have a basic sixth form grasp of medical lingo, you will follow what is being said.

Publications Billions of words have been written about AIDS. This section brings you writing from some of the best and most famous US groups, like Gay Men's Health Crisis and the Women Alive Coalition.

US Government Statistics and the odd damn lie, no doubt. There's an AIDS daily summary, the CDC fact sheets, surveillance reports – the lot, in other words.

Living With HIV Everything. Diet, drugs, alternative treatments, sex, therapy, vitamins, illness, illegal drugs, life insurance, mortgages, discrimination, the science of it all, networks and groups, those funny blood tests; whatever you want, it's here.

An outstanding site with unparalleled information, presented carefully and sensitively.

www.aidsmap.com
AIDS MAP

overall rating:	★ ★ ★ ★ ★
classification:	health
updated:	constant
navigation:	★ ★ ★ ★ ★
content:	★ ★ ★ ★ ★
readability:	★ ★ ★ ★ ★
speed:	★ ★ ★ ★ ★
UK	

This excellent, brilliantly designed site is thoroughly recommended. AIDS MAP comes from the people behind the giant National Aids Manual, published annually, which is packed with information about HIV and AIDS, including history, transmission information and detailed information on safer and unsafe sex choices. The website, funded by UNAIDS and The Elton John AIDS Foundation, is best used with the latest copy of the Manual, which it updates online between its annual printings. Print out the site map first and have a look at what you need, or search using the site's unusually intelligent search engine (it's so refreshing not to get the Spice Girls' homepage when you're only looking for information on buying organic rosemary, don't you think?). You can order NAM publications from the online store, get a list of all UK clinics if you wish to take the HIV test, learn about AIDS organisations worldwide, or get news emailed to you.

Everything on the site comes from the NAM, and it provides you with up-to-date fact sheets on drugs, easy to understand practical information about them, reports from major conferences, and links to hundreds of other sites, often on the same day. There's good information on alternative and complementary therapies, and up-to-date reviews of medical therapies and treatment of opportunistic infections.

SPECIAL FEATURES

The Wheel The Wheel is a Personal Pill Planner designed for anyone taking combination therapy or HAART (highly active antiretroviral therapy). Images of all the current licensed drugs are shown, and you check the ones you are taking. The Wheel then gives you a 24-hour guide to when you should take them, along with information on when and what you should eat. You can print this out and, presumably, stick it on the fridge. Taking the drugs can be confusing, especially at first, and The Wheel helps you rise to it with a better sense of organisation.

Treatment Database Let's face it, there's too much information these days. Inside your head, dear overwhelmed person, you not only have information about all those licensed drugs, the four classifications of drug, their interactions and side effects, and the debate about when to start swallowing them; you also have the current 32 storylines from EastEnders, the whole of Madonna's discography and this week's 74 new special offers from Sainsbury's. You need help, and here's where you get it. Click on Starting Treatment, Changing Treatment, Body Fat Changes, Side Effects and Symptoms to banish confusion.

News Headlines With about 500 HIV and AIDS studies on the go at any one time, even the brightest doctor on the block isn't going to know about the new study in Beirut which shows that laughing 24 times a day lowers your viral load by six per cent – AIDS MAP might. News Headlines covers everything that's breaking now, and you can go back through the news archive until – you guessed it – you're overwhelmed again and back to asking your mates when Tiffany left EastEnders.

Nutrition Booklet is a nifty guide to eating your greens and ending the panic you experience when you look at the Solgar display in the chemist. Do you really need that Shark's Tooth Foot Paste? No! Do you really need more selenium? Yes! This excellent document goes into food and water safety, the relationship between treatment and eating habits, the causes of weight loss, and advice on vitamin overdosing. I found the advice on steroids to be unusually sensible, and NAM is to be congratulated for that alone.

A brilliant site for everyone who wants to learn about HIV.

overall rating: ★ ★ ★ ★ ★	
classification: health	
updated: daily	
navigation: ★ ★ ★ ★ ★	
content: ★ ★ ★ ★ ★	
readability: ★ ★ ★ ★ ★	
speed: ★ ★ ★ ★ ★	
US	

www.thebody.com
The Body

One of the first noticeable aspects of this site is that it has won lots of awards, and that it is sponsored by the pharmaceutical giants Merck and Dupont, among others. The site is vast – even the What's New section contained 30 linked articles when we looked at it. The Body offers a forum where you can submit questions to doctors, and links to just about every HIV-themed publication in the world. The site is an enormous resource, and one of its amazing features is the simplicity of the homepage, which only offers three sections. However, these three sections have got the whole thing covered. It's a little masterpiece of web design, and considering that the topic is not much of a laugh, it's also surprisingly enjoyable to use.

SPECIAL FEATURES

Insight from Experts This is excellent; quite simply, the site has selected an expert doctor in the HIV field to answer your questions. The site divides into forums such as Viral Load and Resistance Testing or Opportunistic Infections. You enter the forum, post your question, read about the doctor, and look at the question and answer cycles of others. There were easily 200 questions answered in the Viral Load Forum when we visited, all of them asked within the last month. There was something about the urgency and reality of the questions that made me retain more of what I had read than if I had read it dry on an information site. All the same, the doctor had to restrict himself to the most general advice, and some people seemed to be trying to get something from the site that it was not designed to give.

Fact of the Day Always a surprise. For example, did you know that there are 16,000 new HIV infections a day? That 30 per cent of sex workers in Cambodia are infected? Changes every day.

Site Map The site map of The Body is vast, and undoubtedly the best place to understand the site. Starting with the simplest things, such as What is AIDS? and Who Gets AIDS?, the site goes on to discuss in depth every single drug, all the complications you might encounter, experimental drugs and alternative therapies, conference coverage, financial issues, legal issues, depression – you name it, it's here, discussed. The wealth of information is phenomenal. For example, choose to read information about a reverse transcriptase inhibitor like d4t and you'll find 30 articles grouped together, all of which put this drug under the microscope.

A rich, detailed site offering the most up-to-date information, with a genuinely interactive feel.

overall rating: ★ ★ ★ ★ ★
classification: health
updated: constant
navigation: ★ ★ ★ ★ ★
content: ★ ★ ★ ★ ★
readability: ★ ★ ★ ★ ★
speed: ★ ★ ★ ★ ★
US

www.healingwell.com
The Healing Well

Healing Well is not just for those suffering from HIV. It's a huge online resource for more or less every kind of disease. You'll find, for example, a whole resource site on Crohn's disease, Migraines, Depression and Prostate Cancer. Each section has its own features, articles, library, bookstore and community, where you can chat to fellow sufferers or post a message on the board. There is no limit to what the articles consider: magnetic cure for migraine, anyone? Olive leaf extract for HIV? Fortunately, and since each disease is dealt with separately, the site is never overwhelming. Only a handful of articles appear in each feature section at any one time. Healing Well deals with every disease and, since the format is the same for every one, you'll find it easy to use once you get used to it. The design is calming; you can see straight away how to find a disease, email your point of view, or search either the site or the whole web. If only Microsoft would do the same on their site! Since this is a US site, you will sometimes be taken somewhere where you have to enter a state and zip code. Here's a tip for Brit surfers: your state is California (CA), and your zip code is 90210. Works every time.

SPECIAL FEATURES

Directory Do you know what Lyme disease is? You can find out here. The directory gives a comprehensive list of all possible kinds of illnesses, how they work and what you can do about them. The directory is the site's list of resources for each disease, and it is organised so that you can find what you want nice and quickly. Click on the HIV section and you'll be taken to a new page packed with links, books on HIV, the chat room and this month's feature articles. At the time of review, these included a piece on dealing with negativity and a charming insight into the help algae can give to sufferers from HIV.

Bookstore The bookstore link takes you to Amazon.com, and you can buy these titles at vastly reduced delivery charges at Amazon.co.uk. The advantage is that Healing Well have listed everything Amazon are offering on the disease in question. They also pick out an editor's choice, to help you choose.

Library The library lists free articles and information about the disease, highlighting the new entries. All the articles are brief and easy to print out, and after a while you get to know the writers and who you respond to.

Medical News Usefully, the site gathers all the late-breaking news together. I reviewed it on August 11th, and it was already featuring information from a study conducted at the University of North Carolina which argues that denial speeds progression to AIDS. That's a fast turnaround, and it wasn't the only article the site had picked up. You can click to email articles to friends, print them, or sign up for a free newsletter. Some of the studies make for comical reading, and you could happily take them to a party. For example: 'Marijuana does not appear to alter viral loads in patients taking protease inhibitors.' Cool, man!

An excellent resource for all diseases, not just HIV.

overall rating: ★ ★ ★ ★ ★	
classification: AIDS advocacy organisation	
updated: monthly	
navigation: ★ ★ ★ ★ ★	
content: ★ ★ ★ ★ ★	
readability: ★ ★ ★ ★ ★	
speed: ★ ★ ★ ★ ★	
UK	

www.nat.org.uk
National Aids Trust

NAT, the National AIDS Trust, is the UK's leading AIDS advocacy organisation. The organisation has a mission, and it's 'to promote a wider understanding of HIV and AIDS, to develop and support efforts to prevent the spread of HIV, and to improve the quality of life of people affected by HIV and AIDS'. The page opens with What's New at NAT, giving an overview of the policy documents they have published and what else they're up to. At the time of writing, NAT had just merged with Red Ribbon International and were promoting the red ribbon appeal, to which you can donate online.

SPECIAL FEATURES

Policy A major component of the NAT's work is its constant campaigning to alter (it would say 'improve', and why not?) public policy on HIV and AIDS. At the time of writing, a number of documents were available to browse online or download in PDF format. These included a joint response, with THT, to a Sexual Health Strategy questionnaire, another entitled, 'Are Health Authorities Failing Gay Men?', and a commissioned report about what the UK must do to reduce the 3,000 new, annual cases of HIV, half of which occur among gay men. NAT lists its policy staff, who you can contact by email, and the reports make for provocative reading, focusing as they do on deficiencies in the system.

Vaccines Up to 100 million people are expected to become infected with HIV over the next 10 years, and 95 per cent of them in developing countries. A vaccine would therefore help. The NAT site offers a comprehensive Vaccines Update which brings together information from vaccine trials, reports from the International Development Committee Enquiry into HIV and Social and Economic Development, and the NAT's own take on vaccine development. The whole process is beset with problems and confusion, not the least of which is limited funding and the commitment to finding a vaccine coming late in the day from major governments. As the NAT site observes, although HIV was identified as the cause of AIDS in 1983 to 1984, the first full-scale efficacy trial for a vaccine did not begin until 1998.

Impact The aim of Impact, the NAT's quarterly policy bulletin, is to bring you the latest news and to generate debate. If you can spare the colour printer ink, you can download all the issues (Impact began in June 1998) and print them out. Issue eight, the most recent, carried features on Section 28 and young people and HIV, including a vaccines update. It is well written and well put together, and I found it most enjoyable to be able to print out a whole magazine, in colour, online. Now there's an unexplored marketing idea.

World AIDS Day World AIDS Day is officially recognised as 1st December. The World AIDS Day project is the result of a partnership between NAT and the Health Education Authority, and in 1999 it focused on children and young people. As the site continually reminds us, last year saw the largest increase in HIV infection rates since records began, and the AIDS Day project is a way of keeping HIV in the spotlight all year round. This is no easy task with a media which moves as fast as ours, and clearly many people are behaving as if the threat of AIDS has gone away. It hasn't, and the NAT's job is to tell you that in as many different ways as it can think of. Put that red ribbon on!

Princess Diana Diana was the Patron of NAT from 1991 until her death in 1997. This moving section of the site tells the story of the work she did on AIDS, which has never really been equalled by any other famous person. Even now, in a hostile and prejudiced world, the sight of her ungloved hands on patients still seems vivid and beautiful. Just reading this makes you realise how many people in positions of power in this country steer clear of the HIV and AIDS issue, pretend it isn't happening and do just about nothing about it. Rarely a democracy, Britain is more of a hypocrisy. Diana challenged that, and she remains a strange and contrary ray of light in the misery of modern life.

A well-executed site giving information on some of the most prominent elements of HIV campaigning: World AIDS Day, the Red Ribbon, and Diana, Princess of Wales.

www.gmhp.demon.co.uk
Gay Men's Health, Wiltshire and Swindon

It might seem a bit strange to go to Swindon to learn about Men's Health, but the surprising thing is that this site offers one of the best guides to coming out that you can find online. It also offers resources for GPs and, if you happen to live in Wiltshire, you can fill in an online form and send for free condoms, lube and leaflets.

SPECIAL FEATURES

Directory is a comprehensive guide to organisations throughout the UK, and links to websites.

Guides offers a guide to coming out, a guide for GPs dealing with homosexual patients, and a guide for health care professionals. They are all well written and concise, and they can either be read online or downloaded in a zip file.

STDs An excellent, online guide to sexually transmitted diseases, symptoms and treatments.

An excellent regional site.

overall rating: ★ ★ ★ ★
classification: gay men's health site
updated: continuous
navigation: ★ ★ ★ ★ ★
content: ★ ★ ★ ★ ★
readability: ★ ★ ★ ★ ★
speed: ★ ★ ★ ★ ★
UK

overall rating:	★ ★ ★ ★
classification:	health
updated:	constant reliability
navigation:	★ ★ ★ ★ ★
content:	★ ★ ★ ★ ★
readability:	★ ★ ★ ★
speed:	★ ★ ★ ★ ★

UK

www.phls.co.uk
Public Health

This is an interesting one! In their words: 'The Public Health Laboratory Service (PHLS) protects the population from infection by detecting, diagnosing, and monitoring communicable diseases. It provides evidence for action to prevent and control infectious disease threats to individuals and populations. The evidence comes from expert analysis and assessment of data generated from the PHLS's own microbiological and epidemiological investigations and from many other sources.'

What makes the site excellent is that it provides a true insight into the complex network which kicks into life the minute someone walks into a GP's surgery with a mysterious illness. Bet you didn't know about the labs up and down the country which carry out tests on samples, and the NHS departments which make the decisions about what is going on, write the press releases and make sure everyone knows. After reading this I felt genuinely moved and completely unable to complain any longer about the lack of available beds.

SPECIAL FEATURES

News and Events At the time of writing, the PHLS was talking about drug-resistant tuberculosis in North London (who knew??), and an odd tummy bug that was infecting tourists returning from Majorca. News and events tells you exactly what is going on in terms of how you catch the bug, how to avoid it, where the outbreak is, how it is treated and what they're doing about it. In this week's section they even said which Majorcan resort was causing the problem, who was coming back with it (a dozen Scottish people), and what they had done about it. Perhaps someone on a hen night had gone too far.

Disease Facts Like the Healing Well site, this site offers information on every disease. It insists, in a brutal blue type, that 'HIV is the cause of AIDS', commenting on the recent South African disputes. PDF files abound here, so download the latest acrobat reader from the site. Whereas another type of site will tell you about the effect of reflexology on AIDS progression, this is a no-nonsense site containing bona-fide Department of Health documents and transmission statistics which are based on solid science, not faith healing. It is interesting to learn about surveillance methods. You may not have known that, by looking at other sexually transmitted diseases, the PHLS can estimate the number of undetected HIV cases.

Publications Find out about the PHLS's operating procedures, and read the surveys about, for example, surgical site infection rates, annual reports and assorted sundry items on communicable diseases.

A quirky site which offers information which you might have thought would be confidential.

overall rating: ★ ★ ★ ★	
classification: political group	
updated: monthly	
navigation: ★ ★ ★ ★ ★	
content: ★ ★ ★ ★ ★	
readability: ★ ★ ★	
speed: ★ ★ ★ ★ ★	
UK	

www.stonewall.org.uk
Stonewall Home Page

It's impossible not to have heard of Stonewall, the national campaigning group, which works for legal equality and social justice for lesbians, gay men and bisexuals. Formed in 1988, Stonewall have fought to put equality on the mainstream political agenda. Their website is a pilot project designed to provide as many people as possible with access to their information service. You can determine what user type suits you (gay man, press, young person, teacher, or whatever) and thereby tailor the site to your needs.

SPECIAL FEATURES

Choose: The site divides into several sections, such as Home, Love, Work and School. Each section then discusses current issues within that area. The 'real issues, real lives' segment of the section features responses from people who are dealing with these problems. The sections are short and sum up the issues, and the campaign areas are further divided. For example, the school campaign has further sections on Section 28, bullying and sex education.

Support Stonewall Make a donation to Stonewall.

About Stonewall A brief history of the organisation and a description of the 1969 riots which gave it its name.

An excellent guide to this important organisation.

www.demon.co.uk/gmfa
GMFA Home Page

overall rating:	★ ★ ★
classification:	AIDS charity
updated:	monthly
navigation:	★ ★ ★ ★ ★
content:	★ ★ ★ ★ ★
readability:	★ ★ ★
speed:	★ ★ ★ ★ ★
UK	

GMFA, or Gay Men Fighting AIDS, is the Brixton-based, long-running and long-campaigning organisation committed to getting gay men to use condoms in sex. It's not an easy thing to do, as the continuing rise in HIV infections shows. So, GMFA are the people who took glowboxes up to the Heath and Finsbury Park to hand out to men who are cruising, and they are the ones who have done masses of work in bars, produced loads of advertising and put together workshops about all manner of relevant issues. Can't handle cruising? Go to their workshop on cruising skills. Don't feel in charge of your HIV treatment? Go to their course called Owning Your Treatment. It all might sound a bit basic and uncool, but it is clearly necessary and, as far as cruising goes, of all the gay men I know, even the most appealing don't often pull hot guys. Swallow your pride and check out this site, which outlines everything that GMFA do.

The design – nude pics, denim stripes and condom click-boxes – might be in dire need of redecoration, but don't let that put you off. Full address and contact details are here, and GMFA love feedback, even if it's negative. The best bit of the site at the moment is Drug Bust, a fast look at the relationship between raw sex and even rawer regret. What I admire about GMFA is that they don't really care if you come away from this site thinking, 'God, why does it have to be like this, we're all trapped, why can't we just FUCK??' That's exactly what they're trying to get you to think: how the hell do you handle living through a sex nightmare? Being nice never saved anyone's life, so why tiptoe politely around the issues? There's plenty here on STDs, including where the clinics are and what safer sex really is. Just click on the coloured handkerchief of your choice.

SPECIAL FEATURES

Own Your Treatment One of the best-written online guides to HIV. You can read this in the time it takes to drink a cup of coffee. The constant exhortation to own your treatment is GMFA's attempt to tell you that you do not have to take a back seat here. Take charge, sit your doctor down and, when you get home, smash the crockery until you begin to feel your power return. Further written information packs are available from GMFA.

Volunteer Find out what you can do for GMFA. You could write for F***sheet, lead workshops, work on the website or hand out condoms on the Heath. You do get a break. There's full information on the Saturday induction courses, an application form and information about restrictions; for example, you need to be in Greater London to join in.

F***sheet This monthly free paper is usually full of news about AIDS, HIV and the changing face of the epidemic. The featured articles can be found online, and GMFA presents information concisely and well, often with instructive graphs. Selected articles from issues going back to 1997 are available.

A thorough site giving a clear picture of what GMFA is all about.

www.harmsen.net/heal/index.html
Heal AIDS

overall rating:	★ ★ ★
classification:	HIV dissident site
updated:	weekly
navigation:	★ ★ ★ ★ ★
content:	★ ★ ★ ★ ★
readability:	★ ★ ★
speed:	★ ★ ★ ★ ★
CAN	

This Toronto-based site offers its own 'Alternative AIDS test', looking at toxicity, a network of support agencies all over the world, and a host of general holistic techniques which would help anyone recover their health, whether they're HIV positive or not. The design is stimulating and the information is presented clearly and directly; no punches are pulled. The site recommends books and links, analyses the safe sex campaigns and, most interestingly, explores the psychological impact of diagnosis and the 'programming to die', which may be as harmful as any physical condition. There is some thought-provoking material about toxic lifestyle and toxic thinking, which is not only trendy but also feels like common sense in a way that swallowing a protease inhibitor never will. The 'Use a Condom' approach to sexual health is also dissected and analysed, and the possibility of getting a falsely positive HIV test is looked at. It's all interesting stuff, well-presented, well-linked and worth a visit. If you recall that everyone thought the world was flat until 500 years ago, and think of how slowly knowledge about reality develops, you might wonder whether the current state of knowledge has the HIV and AIDS phenomenon down.

SPECIAL FEATURES

Who Is Heal? Background on the site, which was founded in 1982 to challenge 'the validity of the HIV/AIDS hypothesis and the efficacy of HIV-based treatment protocols. For more than a decade, HEAL New York has been the leading source for comprehensive information on effective, non-toxic and holistic approaches to recovery from AIDS defining illnesses and has served as a consistent voice calling for honesty in AIDS issues'.

The Controversy This section outlines the mystery of why HIV is so hard to find in patients, even those who have developed AIDS-related symptoms. It features a series of powerful articles from dissenting scientists, each of which can be easily downloaded, printed and read. To some people the controversy is massive, a gigantic mistake made by the medical establishment, but to most doctors that is absolutely ridiculous. They just think HIV causes AIDS, simple as that.

The Aids Tests This section presents information on the chance of false positive tests, the reason why doctors test for antibodies, and evidence that non-positive people might test positive for other reasons. The mystery deepens, or does it?

Africa And The Third World Africa offers the world a unique picture on AIDS: its straight population is by far the largest infected group. But then, to diagnose AIDS in Africa, no HIV test is needed. This means that many traditional African diseases, which are pandemic in poverty stricken areas with a tropical climate, open latrines and contaminated drinking water, might be grouped as AIDS when they are not AIDS.

Does HIV Exist? What if everything you thought about AIDS was wrong? This article, by Christine Maggiore, is one of many on the site which set out to question the idea that HIV even exists.

Surviving And Thriving Why do long-term survivors exist? What are they doing differently? If HIV is so destructive, why doesn't everyone have the same disease progression, as is the case with tuberculosis or measles? Articles in this section unravel these mysteries and suggest new answers. There is also growing evidence that toxic drug treatments, and not HIV itself, kill patients, while continuing use of recreational drugs, cigarettes and alcohol promote poor health for anyone who uses them.

Overall, HEAL, like VIRUSMYTH, is one of the best places to begin for the next part of the debate. It's home to the sceptics and dissenters, those who believe that even if HIV causes AIDS there is much you can do to rearrange your health, and that being a long-term non-progressor doesn't have to mean taking heaps of drugs. Worth a look, if only to get a hold on the complexity of everything that has been said about HIV and AIDS so far.

overall rating: ★ ★ ★
classification: AIDS charity
updated: monthly
navigation: ★ ★ ★ ★ ★
content: ★ ★ ★ ★ ★
readability: ★ ★ ★ ★
speed: ★ ★ ★ ★ ★
UK

www.london-lighthouse.org.uk
London Lighthouse

Backed by a bevy of famous patrons and with 14 years' experience in dealing with the nightmare of AIDS, London Lighthouse is among the most famous of the London charities. The website is respectfully low-key and direct, offering all the necessary information and advice.

SPECIAL FEATURES

Lighthouse History How it all began, back in 1986, and what the aims and strategies of the organisation are now.

Advice Centre Lighthouse has support groups for everyone, from HIV+ gay men and women and those caring for them to an African Men's support group. It has partnerships with other groups so it can point you in the right direction if it can't give you the service you need.

Events Fill your acrobat reader up with the latest news on what they're up to.

Services HIV opens a lot of doors! If you are negative you're not having any of these fab things at Lighthouse: nutrition advice, internet training, yoga classes, massage, reiki, aromatherapy and loads more. Cool.

Respect: 14 years on, and with a solid website to boot.

www.tht.org.uk
The Terence Higgins Trust

The Terence Higgins Trust is Europe's largest HIV charity. The design of this site is a bit cumbersome, but it feels churlish to criticise an organisation which has done so much, helping 12,000 individuals (nearly half the UK total) to live with HIV in 1999. Details of the helpline are online, along with information about what THT is doing at the moment, and its latest campaigns. There's an excellent introduction to their Assume Nothing campaign, designed to get you thinking more clearly about what you're doing or more likely not doing in bed. You might be surprised, however, at what they are doing; for example, inviting you to film premieres (the Mike Figgis flick Timecode), and to The Bloxham Galleries to look at art work by David Hutter. At the moment, there's also a chance to have your say about the proposed THT merger with London Lighthouse. Incidentally, at the time of writing, the Library at THT was closed for refurbishment; call them for more information.

SPECIAL FEATURES

Gay Men is a very fresh resource. THT are here to tell you about their new Face 2 Face campaign, which offers one-to-one advice to gay men, their new Homophobia Campaign, and to report on the conference in Ottawa. In this section they ask, 'Is the AIDS crisis over for urban gay men?', arguing that AIDS does not occupy the central place in gay men's consciousness that it did in the 1980s, and that treatment centres should respond

overall rating:
★ ★ ★

classification:
AIDS charity

updated:
monthly

navigation:
★ ★ ★ ★

content:
★ ★ ★ ★ ★

readability:
★ ★ ★ ★

speed:
★ ★ ★ ★ ★

UK

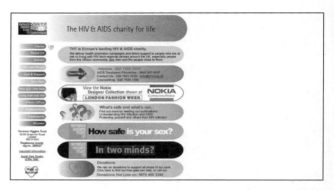

accordingly. They ask – with the total number of AIDS deaths plummeting from nearly 1,700 in 1995 to less than 400 in 1998 – what position does HIV play in the lives of gay men in London? With the effects of smoking killing an estimated 12,000 gay men a year, should the focus of health promotion work be shifting? And are the AIDS organisations the right places for this work to happen? On this page you can also view the latest newsletter and follow the link to CHAPS.

News Download publications (like 'changing combination') and find out about the latest changes in services at THT – or get a cheap phone call deal! Here you can join the mailing list, let them know that you would like to volunteer, and find out about campaigns that are due to be launched.

Treatments THT publishes its treatment briefings online. These documents can be challenging and full of medical jargon, but they are worth reading if you want to find out about side effects, drug interactions and the other treats of being HIV positive. The documents are true briefings, meaning that they draw on all the known, new information at the time and sort it out for you to read. In other words, you don't have to compare studies yourself because they've done it for you. There's good information on vaccines, on joining a clinical trial and on managing HIV treatment, along with a host of links to other pages.

Policy Read the THT's policies on matters like disclosing HIV status, taking the antibody test and testing for pregnant women. In these sensitive areas, THT have established a set of guidelines which they refer to when giving advice.

Women THT produces a number of publications specifically for women. It also has several services, including advice about benefits and housing, legal advice and buddying, and advice about treatments.

A high-quality, informative site which lives up to the expectations people have of THT.

overall rating: ★ ★ ★
classification: HIV dissident site
updated: continuous
navigation: ★ ★ ★ ★ ★
content: ★ ★ ★ ★ ★
readability: ★ ★ ★
speed: ★ ★ ★ ★ ★
US

www.virusmyth.com
Virus Myth

'If there is evidence that HIV causes AIDS, there should be scientific documents which either singly or collectively demonstrate that fact, at least with a high probability. There is no such document.' So says Kary Mullis, Biochemist, 1993 Nobel Prize for Chemistry, on the opening page of this site, which collects the most polished of the dissenting articles about HIV and AIDS. It is well organised and, due to its attack on orthodox thinking, a compulsive site. Scientific observations are combined with a storytelling technique which ensures the reader doesn't get lost or irritated. Visually it's spare, but you don't want Shockwave on a site this serious. You just want to know what these people mean when they say HIV is harmless. Almost all of the hundreds of documents I looked at were clearly, effectively written. Loading was fast, navigation is easy and the site rarely becomes overwhelming, which is an achievement on a site with one-million words of text to share. One slight downside: there is a great deal of repetition, and most writers make similar points.

SPECIAL FEATURES

Introduction Scan this list of documents and you get the general idea: 'Fatal Distraction', 'Conspiracy of Silence', 'HIV, reality or artefact?' and 'How much longer can we afford the AIDS Virus Monopoly?' But these introductory documents, which present the main arguments against the 'HIV causes AIDS' theory, are hardly the work of crackpots. Peter Duesburg, whose interview appears here, is the Professor of Molecular Biology at Berkeley, and one of the world's leading experts on retroviruses. You can download the whole of the introduction in a convenient zip file before you go into the other sections of the page.

Tour Takes you through the history: gay men get sick in New York, LA and San Francisco; the US Health Secretary announces that Robert Gallo has discovered why, and the fight to beat HIV began. Everyone was told to wear condoms. Everyone was given AZT. Somehow, during the 1990s, the survival rate of people diagnosed HIV positive rocketed from three years to 12 years. Protease inhibitors came along and now, 15 years and one-hundred-billion dollars later, still no-one knows how to kick AIDS out of its position as the leading cause of death for Western men aged 25-44. The tour skims the established principles of virology and immunology, wonders why the heterosexual AIDS explosion never happened, and reminds us that HIV testing has no gold standard. The site offers a £1,000 reward to anyone who can isolate the virus (the prize remains unclaimed), and lists scientists around the world who form the Group for the Scientific Reappraisal of the HIV-AIDS Hypothesis. The upside-down ribbon logo is pretty cool. Turn yours over today.

Audio And Video Documentaries Television and radio documentaries which question the conventional HIV/AIDS hypothesis, some of them censored.

To sum up, this is a huge site which provokes thought and really does make you wonder.

OTHER SITES OF INTEREST

Positive Nation
www.positivenation.co.uk
Positive Nation magazine is published each month in print. It aims to provide a platform for all people who are affected by HIV and AIDS in the UK. It's got the best links page I've seen, and you can read every magazine online, go through the archive, make contact or subscribe using your credit card. A cool, colourful design and a warm, simple approach to AIDS and HIV.

AIDS Education & Research Trust (AVERT)
www.avert.org
A neatly designed site, with 18 subsections ranging from a history of HIV to Treatment and Healthcare, Sex, AIDS and relationships, and links. The history section is clear and well-written. It's hard to criticise anything about the site, which succeeds in its aim to raise awareness among young people.

AIDS Treatment News (ATN)
www.immunet.org/atn
AIDS Treatment News offers a complete archive of documents and you can search the site easily enough. I found the Durban Conference Official Webcast pretty amazing, and you can also find the complete 'Durban Declaration', and the list of signatories, on here.

Journal of the American Medical Association
www.ama-assn.org/special/hiv
Reuters Health information service powers this constantly updated US site. Choose from a news line, treatment centre,

prevention information and best of the net; alternatively, search for what you want or give feedback.

Medscape
http://hiv.medscape.com/Home/Topics/AIDS/AIDS.html
This site is aimed mainly at doctors, but it also carries the latest conference summaries. It's a scientific site which assumes that you know your HIV basics, but with a bit of patience it yields rewards. Still, you will have to want to get your teeth into articles entitled 'Peripherally Inserted Central Catheters Safe for AIDS Patients'. Are you ready for this?

Peter Duesburg's site
www.duesberg.com
This site is the home of AIDS dissident Peter Duesburg. It reiterates most of what is said on the other dissident sites, but you should note that few substantial articles have been added since 1996. The site is of historical interest and does ask a number of as yet unanswered questions about HIV and AIDS.

About: AIDS
http://aids.about.com/health/aids/
A very friendly and informal site, this is part of the huge 'about' resource, which has over 700 sites. The 'In the Spotlight' section provides the latest news, including important warnings on drugs, new information about HIV and AIDS, and information on other STDs. The subjects looked at on the site are posted in a simple list, and basically cover everything within the site's remit. I enjoyed the frank, open style, fast navigation and common-sense presentation of information.

DAAIR
http://www.daair.org/DAAIR/MEMBINFO.NSf
This site is the place to purchase complementary therapies online. If you think you need wheat grass juice, B12, mega vitamin C or whatever else, you can order it, read about it and understand it here.

OutZone
www.outzone.org
An excellent UK page with information on safer sex, HIV and AIDS, sexual health clinics, coming out, assertivenesss and the latest gay films and TV shows. Funded by Enfield and Haringey Health Authority and Haringey Council, OutZone is designed to spend money on HIV Prevention – and it's doing a fine job.

Wellness Healthcare Information Resources
http://www-hsl.mcmaster.ca/tomflem/gay.html
Massive links site from Wellness Health Care Information Resources, with links to numerous gay and lesbian health sites.

Lesbian, Gay and Bisexual Health Science Librarians
http://www.uic.edu/~shaffer/mlalgb/
This site catalogues links to libraries, articles and health sites, dividing into lesbian health, gay men's health, mental health, HIV and AIDS.

Gay Men's Health Summit
http://www.temenos.net/summit
This site, from Boulder, Colorado, offers information on gay men's health summits in progress. It's got links, articles, galleries and more.

GayHealth

http://www.gayhealth.com

A large and well-written site focusing mainly on HIV, with a news service, information about food, fitness, emotional health, sex and drugs.

Noah

http://www.noah-health.org/index.html

NOAH is the New York Online Access to Health page. Written in Spanish and English, it features a large number of articles about many different health issues. Not merely a HIV and AIDS page, this page carries information about all health problems.

Gay and Lesbian Health Issues

http://www.omsa.uiuc.edu/clearinghouse/gaylesbian/ gay.html

This health page is directed at the health concerns and needs of ethnic communities, and focuses on African American Health issues, Asian American health issues, Native American Health and Latino Health. It also has sections on students with disabilities and women. As you would expect, a large section on HIV dominates the site.

glossary of internet terms

A

Accelerators Add-on programs, which speed up browsing.

Acceptable Use Policy These are the terms and conditions of using the internet. They are usually set by organisations, who wish to regulate an individual's use of the internet. For example, an employer might issue a ruling on the type of email which can be sent from an office.

Access Provider A company which provides access to the internet, usually via a dial-up account. Many companies such as AOL and Dircon charge for this service, although there are an increasing number of free services such as Freeserve, Lineone and Tesco.net. Also known as an Internet Service Provider.

Account A user's internet connection, with an Access/ Internet Service Provider, which usually has to be paid for.

Acrobat Reader Small freely-available program, or web browser plug-in, which lets you view a Portable Document Format (PDF) file.

Across Lite Plug-in which allows you to complete crossword puzzles online.

Address Location name for email or internet site, which is the online equivalent of a postal address. It is usually composed of a unique series of words and punctuation, such as *my.name@myhouse.co.uk.*

See also URL.

America Online (AOL) World's most heavily subscribed online service provider.

Animated GIF Low-grade animation technique used on websites.

ASCII Stands for American Standard Code for Information Interchange, It is a coding standard which all computers can recognise, and ensures that if a character is entered on one part of the internet, the same character will be seen elsewhere.

ASCII Art Art made of letters and other symbols. Because it is made up of simple text, it can be recognised by different computers.

ASDL Stands for Asynchronous Digital Subscriber Line, which is a high speed copper wire which will allow rapid transfer of information. Not widely in use at moment, though the government is pushing for its early introduction.

Attachment A file included with an email, which may be composed of text, graphics and sound. Attachments are encoded for transfer across the internet, and can be viewed in their original form by the recipient. An attachment is the equivalent of putting a photograph with a letter in the post.

B

Bookmark A function of the Netscape Netvigator browser which allows you to save a link to your favourite web pages, so that you can return straight there at a later date, without having to re-enter the address. Favourites in internet Explorer is the same thing.

BPS Abbreviation of Bits Per Second, which is a measure of the speed at which information is transferred or downloaded.

Browse Common term for looking around the web. See also Surfing.

Browser A generic term for the software that allows users to move and look around the Web. Netscape Navigator and Internet Explorer are the ones that most people are familiar with, and they account for 97 percent of web hits.

Bulletin Board Service A BBS is a computer with a telephone connection, which allows you direct contact to upload and download information and converse with other users, via the computer. It was the forerunner to the online services and virtual communities of today.

C

Cache A temporary storage space on the hard drive of your computer, which stores downloaded websites. When you return to a website, information is retrieved from the cache and displayed much more rapidly. However, this information may not be the most recent version for sites which are frequently updated and you will need to reload the Website address for these.

Chat Talking to other users on the web in real time, but with typed, instead of spoken words. Special software such as ICQ or MIRC is required before you can chat.

Chat Room An internet channel which allows several people to type in their messages, and talk to one another over the internet.

Clickstream The trail left as you 'click' your way around the web.

Content The material on a website that actually relates to the site, and is hopefully of interest or value. Things like adverts are not considered to be part of the content. The term is also used to refer to information on the internet that can be seen by users, as opposed to programming and other background information.

Cookie A cookie is a nugget of information sometimes sent by websites to your hard drive when you visit.They contain such details as what you looked at, what you ordered, and can add more information, so that the website can be customized to suit you.

Cybercafe Cafe where you can use a computer terminal to browse the net for a small fee.

Cyberspace When first coined by the sci-fi author William Gibson, it meant a shared hallucination which occured when people logged on to computer networks. Now, it refers to the virtual space you're in when on the internet.

D

Dial Up A temporary telephone connection to your ISP's computer and how you make contact with your ISP, each time you log onto the Internet.

Domain The part of an Internet address which identifies an individual computer, and can often be a business or person's name. For example, in the goodwebguide.com the domain name is theGoodWebGuide.

Download Transfer of information from an Internet server to your computer.

Dynamic HTML The most recent version of the HTML standard.

E

Ecash Electronic cash, used to make transactions on the internet.

Ecommerce The name for business which is carried out over the internet.

Email Mail which is delivered electronically over the internet. They are usually comprised of text messages, but can contain illustrations, music and animations. Mail is sent to an email address, which is the internet equivalent of a postal address.

Encryption A process whereby information is scrambled to produce a 'coded message', so that it can't be read whilst in transit on the internet. The recipient must have decryption software in order to read the message.

Expire Term referring to newsgroup postings which are automatically deleted after a fixed period of time.

Ezine Publication on the web, which is updated regularly.

F

FAQ Stands for frequently asked questions and is a common section on websites where the most common enquiries and their answers are archived.

Frame A method which splits web pages into several windows.

FTP/File Transfer Protocol Standard method for transporting files across the internet.

G

GIF/Graphics Interchange Format A format in which graphics are compressed, and a popular method of putting images onto the internet, as they take little time to download.

Gopher The gopher was the precursor of the world wide web and consisted of archives accessed through a menu, usually organised by subject.

GUI/Graphical User Interface. This is the system which turns binary information into the words and images format you can see on your computer screen. For example, instead of seeing the computer language which denotes the presence of your toolbar, you actually see a toolbar.

H

Hackers A term used to refer to expert programmers who used their skills to break into computer systems, just for the fun of it. Nowadays the word is more commonly associated with computer criminals, or Crackers.

Header Basic indication of what's in an email: who it's from, when it was sent, and what it's about.

Hit When a file is downloaded from a website it is referred to as a 'hit'. Measuring the number of hits is a rough method of counting how many people visit a website. Except that it's not wholly accurate as one website can contain many files, so one visit by an individual may generate several hits.

Homepage Most usually associated with a personal site, produced by an individual, but can also refer to the first page on your browser, or the first page of a website.

Host Computer on which a website is stored. A host computer may store several websites, and usually has a fast powerful connection to the internet. Also known as a Server.

HTML/Hypertext Mark-Up Language The computer code used to construct web pages.

HTTP/Hypertext Transfer Protocol The protocol for moving HTML files across the web.

Hyperlink A word or graphic formatted so that when you click on it, you move from one area to another. See also hypertext.

Hypertext Text within a document which is formatted so it acts as a link from one page to another, or from one document to another.

I

Image Map A graphic which contains hyperlinks.

Interface What you actually see on the computer screen.

Internet One or more computers connected to one another is an internet (lower case i). The Internet is the biggest of all the internets. and consists of a worldwide collection of interconnected computer networks.

Internet Explorer One of the most popular pieces of browser software, produced by Microsoft.

Intranet A network of computers, which works in the same way as an internet, but for internal use, such as within a corporation.

ISDN/Integrated Services Digital Network Digital telephone line which facilitates very fast connections and can transfer larges amounts of data. It can carry more than one form of data at once.

ISP/Internet Service Provider See Access Provider.

J

Java Programming language which can be used to create interactive multimedia effects on webpages. The language is used to create programmes known as *applets* that add features such as animations, sound and even games to websites.

Javascript A scripting language which, like Java, can be used to add extra multimedia features. However, in contrast with Java it does not consist of separate programmes. Javascript is embedded into the HTML text and can interpreted by the browser, provided that the user has a javascript enabled browser.

JPEG Stands for 'Joint Photographic Experts Group' and is the name given to a type of format which compresses photos, so that they can be seen on the web.

K

Kill file A function which allows a user to block incoming information from unwanted sources. Normally used on email and newsreaders.

L

LAN/Local Area Network A type of internet, but limited to a single area, such as an office.

Login The account name or password needed to access a computer system.

Link Connection between web pages, or one web document and another, which are accessed via formatted text and graphic.

M

Mailing List A discussion group which is associated with a website. Participants send their emails to the site, and it is copied and sent by the server to other individuals on the mailing list.

Modem A device for converting digital data into analogue signals for transmission along standard phone lines. The usual way for home users to connect to the internet or log into their email accounts. May be internal (built into the computer) or external (a desk-top box connected to the computer).

MP3 A compressed music file format, which has almost no loss of quality although the compression rate may be very high.

N

Netscape Popular browser, now owned by AOL.

Newbie Term for someone new to the Internet. Used perjoratively of newcomers to bulletin boards or chat, who commit the sin of asking obvious questions or failing to observe the netiquette.

Newsgroup Discussion group amongst Internet users who share a mutual interest. There are thousands of newsgroups covering every possible subject.

O

Offline Not connected to the internet via a telephone line.

Online Connected to the internet via a telephone line.

Offline Browsing A function of the browser software, which allows the user to download pages and read them whilst offline.

Online Service Provider Similar to an access provider, but provides addtional features such as live chat.

P

PDF/Portable Document Format A file format created by Adobe for offline reading of brochures, reports and other documents with complex graphic design, which can be read by anyone with Acrobat Reader.

Plug-in Piece of software which adds more functions (such as playing music or video) to another, larger software program.

POP3/Post Office Protocol An email protocol that allows you to pick up your mail from any location.

Portal A website which offers many services, such as search engines, email and chat rooms, and to which people are likely to return to often . ISPs such as Yahoo and Alta Vista provide portal sites which are the first thing you see when you log on, and in theory act as gateways to the rest of the web.

Post/Posting Information sent to a usenet group, bulletin board, message board or by email.

PPP/Point to Point Protocol The agreed way of sending data over dial-up connections, so that the user's computer, the modem and the Internet Server can all recognise it. It is the protocol which allows you to get online.

Protocol Convention detailing a set of actions that computers in a network must follow so that they can understand one another.

Q

Query Request for specific information from a database.

R

RAM /Random Access Memory Your computer's short term memory.
Realplayer G2 A plug-in program that allows you to view video in real-time and listen to sound and which is becoming increasingly

important for web use.

Router A computer program which acts as an interface between two networks, and decides how to route information.

S

Searchable Database A database on a website which allows the user to search for information, usually be keyword.

Search Engine Programs which enable web users to search for pages and sites using keywords. They are usually to be found on portal sites and browser homepages. Infoseek, Alta Vista and Lycos are some of the popular search engines.

Secure Transactions Information transfers which are encrypted so that only the sender and recipient have access to the uncoded message, so that the details within remain private. The term is most commonly used to refer to credit card transactions, although other information can be sent in a secure form.

Server A powerful computer that has a permanent fast connection to the internet. Such computers are usually owned by companies and act as host computers for websites.

Sign-on To connect to the internet and start using one of its facilities.

Shareware Software that doesn't have to be paid for or test version of software that the user can access for free, as a trial before buying it.

Standard A style which the whole of the computer industry has agreed upon. Industry standards mean that hardware and software produced by the various different computer companies will work with one another.

Surfing Slang for looking around the Internet, without any particular aim, following links from site to site.

TLA/Three Letter Acronyms Netspeak for the abbreviations of net jargon, such as BPS (Bits Per Second) and ISP (Internet Service Provider).

Upload To send files from your computer to another one on the internet. When you send an email you are uploading a file.

URL/Uniform Resource Locator Jargon for an address on the internet, such as www.thegoodwebguide.co.uk.

Usenet A network of newsgroups, which form a worldwide system, on which anyone can post 'news'.

Virtual Community Name given to a congregation of regular mailing list/ newsgroup users.

VRML/Virtual Reality Modeling Language Method for creating 3D environments on the web.

Wallpaper Description of the sometimes hectic background patterns which appear behind the text on some websites.

Web Based Email/Webmail Email accounts such as Hotmail and Rocketmail, which are accessed via an Internet browser, rather than an email program such as Outlook Express. Webmail has to be typed whilst the user is online, but can accessed from anywhere on the Web.

Webmaster A person responsible for a web server. May also be known as System Administrator.

Web Page Document which forms one part of a website (though some sites are a single page), usually formatted in HTML.

Web Ring Loose association of websites which are usually dedicated to the same subject and often contain links to one another.

Website A collection of related web pages which often belong to an individual or organisation and are about the same subject.

World Wide Web The part of the Internet which is easy to get around and see. The term is often mistakely interchanged with Internet, though the two are not the same. If the Internet is a shopping mall, with shops, depots, and delivery bays, then the web is the actual shops which the customers see and use.

index

other great titles in thegoodwebguide **series:**

hardback £12.99

genealogy	ISBN 1-903282-06-3
health	ISBN 1-903282-08-x
home	ISBN 1-903282-15-2
museums and galleries	ISBN 1-903282-14-4
travel	ISBN 1-903282-05-5
wine	ISBN 1-903282-04-7

paperback £7.99

food	ISBN 1-903282-17-9
gardening	ISBN 1-903282-16-0
money	ISBN 1-903282-18-7
parents	ISBN 1-903282-19-5

small paperbacks £4.99

comedy	ISBN 1-903282-20-9
games	ISBN 1-903282-10-1
gay life	ISBN 1-903282-13-6
music	ISBN 1-903282-11-x
sex	ISBN 1-903282-09-8
sport	ISBN 1-903282-07-1
tv	ISBN 1-903282-12-8